Proofs of

Existence, and Dangerous

Tendency, of Illuminism

Containing an abstract of the most
interesting parts of what Dr. Robison and the
Abbe Barruel have published on this subject,
with collateral proofs and general
observations

Seth Payson

Alpha Editions

This edition published in 2020

ISBN : 9789354030352

Design and Setting By
Alpha Editions
email - alphaedis@gmail.com

PROOFS

OF THE

REAL EXISTENCE, AND DANGEROUS TENDENCY,

OF

ILLUMINISM.

CONTAINING

AN ABSTRACT OF THE MOST INTERESTING PARTS OF
WHAT DR. ROBISON AND THE

ABBE BARRUEL

HAVE PUBLISHED ON THIS SUBJECT ; WITH COLLAT-
ERAL PROOFS AND GENERAL OBSERVATIONS,

BY SETH PAYSON, A. M.

" For they are the Spirits of devils." REV. xvi. 14

———— " Here nature breeds
Perverse, all monstrous, all prodigious things
Abominable, unutterable, and worse
Than fables yet have feign'd, or fear conceiv'd."
MILTON.

Published according to Act of Congress.

Charlestown :

PRINTED BY SAMUEL ETHERIDGE,

FOR THE AUTHOR,

1802,

PREFACE.

THE efforts which have been made to difcredit the exiftence of Illuminifm, and the torrents of
abufe which have been fo liberally poured on fuch as
have attempted, apparently from the pureft motives,
to unveil this myftery of iniquity, have in part produced the end defigned. Some have miftaken vocifer-
ation for argument, and confident affertions for proofs ;
while others have been prevented from publifhing their
belief and their fears, not choofing to encounter the
fhafts of ridicule and defamation ; weapons found to
be of great importance in this *age of reafon*. A general
ftupor has hence taken place of that juft alarm, occa-
fioned by the firft difcovery of this infernal combination.

But has the caufe of alarm ceafed ? There has been
much clamor indeed, but have any folid, fatisfying
proofs been exhibited, either that there has not been,
or is not now exifting, a confpiracy, which has for its
ultimate object, the abolition of chriftianity and government ? Solid proofs alone ought to fatisfy us on a
fubject fo highly interefting to mankind. Such proofs
have not, I confefs, come to my knowledge. Recent
events do, on the contrary, confirm my belief, that a
fyftematical attempt is now in operation to undermine
the foundation of every religious, moral, and focial
eftablifhment. To thofe who have this belief, it muft
appear important that the impending danger be placed
in the moft confpicuous point of view ; that the evi-

dence of this fact, now diffused through expensive, and voluminous tracts, and arising from a variety of circumstances, should be collected into one point, freed from the obscurity in which it has been industriously involved, and the whole comprised in a volume, easy to the purchaser, and intelligible to every reader. The importance of such a publication at the present critical period, and which I have expected, and hoped to see from some abler hand, is all the apology I have to offer for undertaking the task.

To defend religion, by exposing the plots concerted for its destruction, is the principal object of this publication : and if any thing of a political nature is introduced, it is with a view of detecting, and counteracting that dark policy, which has connected the subversion of every good government, with the overthrow of christianity.

I claim no merit for discovering what I could not avoid seeing, but by shutting my eyes ; and I fear no censure, for I have obeyed the call of duty. I have no hope of convincing those who have had access to the evidence here referred to, but for reasons best known to themselves, have rejected it ; nor the many who have presumed to give judgment without examination : this statement of evidence is for those who have no medium of vision ; and those, whose optics have been injured by the dust which sophistry, prejudice, and the powers of darkness have raised. Could I contribute but a mite, which is my all, to preserve my country from that vortex of anarchy, which has ingulphed the liberties, civil and religious, and the peace, property, and lives of millions, my labor will not be unrewarded.

CONTENTS.

Page.

PRELIMINARY OBSERVATIONS, - 5

CHAP. I.
The Actors, Existence, Object, and Secret of the Con-
spiracy, - - - - - 30

II.
The means of the Conspirators, - - - 39

III.
The Progress of the Conspiracy ; Triumph and Death
of the Chiefs, - - - - 55

IV.
Occult Masonry, - - - - - 64

V.
Illuminism ; its Origin, Actors, and different
grades, - - - - - - 81

VI.
Code of the Illuminees, - - - - 89

VII.
The Mysteries and Government of the Order, - 102

VIII.
The Discovery of the Sect, - - - - 115

IX.
German Union, - - - - - 131

CONTENTS.

X.

French Revolution, - - - - 140

XI.

Summary view of Illuminifm, - - - 155

XII.

Objections confidered, - - - - 168

XIII.

Collateral Proofs, and general Obfervations in relation to Europe, - - - 175

XIV.

The fame, in relation to the United States, - 195

XV.

In Continuation, - - - - - 217

An ADDRESS, - - - - - 245

CONCLUSION, - - - - - 286

PRELIMINARY OBSERVATIONS.

To remove the obstructions which prej-
udiced and designing men have raised, is often
a necessary, but laborious and ungrateful task,
attending our inquiries after truth. No sooner
is the precious gem brought to view, than its
enemies, who hate its light, and cannot endure
its brilliancy, are busily employed in covering
it with filth and rubbish ; hence much of the
labor of those who wish to possess the heavenly boon.

The testimony of Professor Robison, and
Abbe Barruel, would doubtless have been considered as ample, in any case which did not
interest the prejudices and passions of men
against them. The scurrility and odium with
which they have been loaded is perfectly natural, and what the nature of their testimony
would have led any one to expect. Men will
endeavor to invalidate that evidence which

A 2

tends to unveil their dark defigns : and it cannot be expected that thofe who believe that
" the end fanctifies the means," will be very
fcrupulous as to their meafures. Certainly he
was not, who invented the following character, and arbitrarily applied it to Dr. Robifon,
which might have been applied with as much
propriety to any other perfon in Europe or
America. The character here referred to, is
taken from the American Mercury, printed at
Hartford, Sept. 26, 1799, by E. Babcock. In
this paper, on the pretended authority of Profeffor Ebeling,* we are told, " That Robifon
had lived too faft for his income, and to fupply deficiencies, had undertaken to alter a bank
bill ; that he was detected, and fled to France ;
that having been expelled the Lodge in Edinburgh, he applied in France for the fecond
grade, but was refufed ; that he made the
fame attempt in Germany, and afterwards in

---

* It is but juftice to the character of Profeffor Ebeling,
to fay, that in none of his Letters to his American Cor-
refpondents, of which I have information, has he given
the leaft intimation that Profeffor Robifon was guilty
of the crimes here imputed to him. Nor has he, to my
knowledge, ever criminated his moral character. Thefe
bafe calumnies originated, not from Mr. Ebeling, but
from a fpirit of malignant oppofition to Dr. Robifon ;
and they furnish ftrong evidence of the truth of his
writings.

Ruflia, but never fucceeded ; and from this
entertained the bitterest hatred to mafonry ;
that after wandering about Europe, for two
years, by writing to Secretary Dundas, and
prefenting a copy of his book, which, it was
judged, would anfwer certain purpofes of the
miniftry, the profecution againft him was ftop-
ped, the Profeffor returned in triumph to his
country, and now lives upon a handfome pen-
fion, inftead of fuffering the fate of his prede-
ceffor Dodd."

A writer, in the *National Intelligencer*, of
Jan. 1801, who ftyles himfelf " A friend to
Truth," and from whom, (if conjecture has
pointed out the real author) better things
ought to have been expected, fpeaks of Dr.
Robifon as " a man diftinguiflied by abject
dependence on a party ; by the bafe crimes of
forgery, and adultery ; and by frequent pa-
roxyfins of infanity."

As Dr. Robifon is a principal evidence in
the caufe now pending, it will be neceffary to
inquire, whether this is indeed a juft view of
the man. The refult of this inquiry, contraft-
ed with the above character, will ferve to give
the public fome idea of the means which have
been made ufe of to difcredit Illuminifm, and

how *benevolently* diſpoſed ſome among us are, to prevent their countrymen from being miſled by what are called, the *ridiculous reveries* of Robiſon. The reader's patience, it is feared, will be exhauſted by the detail of credentials which the effrontery of his accuſers have rendered neceſſary ; but the character of a witneſs is of the firſt importance. The following ſketch of the principal events of the life of Dr. Robiſon, was drawn up from authentic documents, received direct from Edinburgh, through a reſpectable channel.*

" The father of the Profeſſor, a reſpectable country gentleman, intended him for the church, and gave him eight years of an Univerſity education at Glaſgow. Preferring a different profeſſion, he accepted an offer of going into the Navy, with very flattering proſpects. He was appointed Mathematical Inſtructor to his Royal Highneſs the Duke of York. In that office, he accordingly entered the Navy in February, 1759, being that day

* Concerning the facts contained in this hiſtorical ſketch, which were communicated to Dr. Erſkine, he writes thus. " The moſt important facts in it I have had acceſs to know, being firſt ſettled at Kirkintilloch, the neighbouring pariſh to Boderoch, where lay the eſtate of his worthy father. For the few facts of which I know leſs, full and unexceptionable vouchers can be produced."

twenty years old. He was prefent at the fiege
of Quebec. With the late Admiral Knowles,
he was particularly connected, and his fon,
afterwards captain Knowles, one of the moft
promifing young officers in the Britifh Navy,
was committed to his charge.

In 1761, he was fent by the board of Admiralty, to make trial of Harrifon's Watch at Ja-
maica. At the peace of 1763, he returned to
College. In 1764, he was again appointed by
the Admiralty to make trial of Harrifon's
improved Watch at Barbadoes ; but his patron, Lord Anfon, being dead, and the condi-
tions not fuch as pleafed him, he declined the
employment, returned again to College, and
took under his care the only remaining fon of
his friend, Sir Charles Knowles. This fon is
the prefent Admiral Sir Charles Knowles. In
1770, Sir Charles was invited by the Emprefs
of Ruffia to take charge of her Navy. He
took Mr. Robifon with him as his Secretary.
In 1772, Mr. Robifon was appointed fuperin-
tendant of the education in the Marine Caflet
Corps, where he had under his direction about
500 youth, 350 of whom were fons of noble-
men and gentlemen, and 26 mafters in the different ftudies. The Academy being burnt, Mr.
Robifon, with his pupils, removed to an

ancient palace of Peter the Great at Cronſtadt, a moſt miſerable, deſolate iſland, where, finding no agreeable ſociety, he availed himſelf of the firſt opportunity, of quitting ſo unpleaſant a ſituation, and accepted an invitation from the Magiſtrates of Edinburgh, to the Profeſſorſhip of Natural Philoſophy in the Univerſity in that city, which ranks among the firſt Univerſities in the world. To this very honorable office he acceded in Auguſt, 1774, and from that time continued his lectures, without interruption, till 1792, when illneſs obliged him to aſk for an aſſiſtant. To enable him to give ſuch a ſalary to his aſſiſtant, as would make the place worth the acceptance of a man of talents, the King was pleaſed to give him a penſion of £.100 a year. After five years confinement, by a painful diſorder, he reſumed his chair, in 1797.

In 1786, he was elected a member of the Philoſophical Society at Philadelphia, of which Mr. Jefferſon is Preſident; and in 1797, a member of the Royal Society of Mancheſter. In 1799, after the publication of his book, the Univerſity of Glaſgow, where he received his education, conferred on him, unſolicited, the honor of a Doctor's degree in Law, in which, contrary to the uſual cuſtom in theſe caſes, is given a very particular and flattering account of

his nine years studies in that University. This
peculiar evidence of esteem and respect was
given in this way, in order that his Diploma
might have all the civil consequences which
long standing could give. When he published his book, in 1797, he was Secretary of the
Royal Society of Edinburgh. In April, 1800,
without solicitation of a single friend, he was
unanimously elected a Foreign Member (there
are but six) of the Imperial Academy of Sciences, at St. Petersburg, (which, in point of
reputation, is esteemed the third on the con-
tinent of Europe) in the room of the much
lamented and highly celebrated Dr. Black.
To prepare for the press, and superintend the
publication of the Chemical writings of this
great man, required the ablest Chemist in
Great Britain. This distinguished honor has
been conferred on Professor Robison, who has
undertaken this important work. This appointment, for which no man perhaps is more
competent, together with the numerous, learned, and copious articles which he has furnished for the Encyclopedia Brittanica, fully evince
that in reputation and solid learning, he ranks
among the first literary characters in Europe.
Add to all this, *he sustains a* MORAL *character,*
so fair and unblemished, that any man may safely be

*challenged to lay any thing to his charge of which an
honeſt man need be aſhamed.''*

The following account of Profeſſor Robiſon, is from a Work, entitled " Literary Memoirs of Living Authors of Great Britain,
&c." in two volumes, 8vo. publiſhed in London, 1798, for R. Faulder :

" John Robiſon, Eſq. M. A. Secretary to
the Royal Society at Edinburgh, and Profeſ-
for of Natural Philoſophy in the Univerſity.
Profeſſor Robiſon is diſtinguiſhed for his ac-
curate and extenſive knowledge, eſpecially on
ſubjects of ſcience.   He contributed to the
Encyclopedia Brittanica the valuable articles,
Phyſics, Pneumatics, Præceſſion of the Equi-
noxes, Projectiles, Pumps, Reſiſtance of Flu-
ids, River, Roof, Rope making, Rotation,
Seamanſhip, Signals, Sound, Specific Gravity,
Statics, Steam, Steam-Engine, Strength of
Materials, Teleſcope, Tide, Articulating Trum-
pet, Variation of the Compaſs, and Water-
Works, alſo Philoſophy, in aſſociation with
Dr. Gleig.

In the autumn of the year 1797, Profeſſor
Robiſon publiſhed an octavo volume, entitled
" Proofs of a Conſpiracy, &c."   This volume

has been favorably received, and although too hafty a performance for a work of fo much confequence, is well entitled, both from its fubject and its authenticity, to the ferious attention of every reader. It arrives at the fame remarkable conclufion as the celebrated Memoirs of the Abbe Barruel, illuftrating the hiftory of Jacobinifm, though the authors were perfectly unconnected with each other, and purfued their inquiries in very different ways. It has raifed (we are forry for fuch an appearance) a confiderable clamor and enmity againft the Profeffor ; though it was written, we are fully convinced, from the beft of motives. We cannot conclude this article without obferving that the principles, and honeft zeal, which Profeffor Robifon has difplayed upon this occafion, are highly creditable to him, and merit the warmeft acknowledgements from fociety in general."

The following is an extract of a letter from one of the moft refpectable literary characters which Scotland has produced, dated March, 1800. The writer of this letter is now in America. I have not his leave to mention his name.

" Profeffor Robifon's character is fo well eftablifhed among thofe who know him beft,

B

that it would be ridiculous, at Edinburgh, to
call in queſtion his veracity or ability. *I had
read many of his authorities in the German originals
before his book was publiſhed;* and the firſt notice
I received of it was, in the preface to Dr.
Erſkine's ſketches of eccleſiaſtical hiſtory,
where you will ſee the honorable teſtimony
that he gives Mr. Robiſon, and the great ex-
pectation that he had from his publication."

The Rev. Dr. Erſkine, whoſe character is
generally known, and reſpected in America,
and who is a neighbor to Dr. Robiſon, in a
letter, dated Edinburgh, September 25, 1800,
ſays, " I think highly of Profeſſor Robiſon's
book. Some of the moſt ſhocking facts
it contains, I knew before its publication,
from a periodical account of the church hiſtory of the times, by Profeſſor Koeſter at
Gietſen, of which I lent him all the numbers
relating to that ſubject. For three years, that
valuable work has been diſcontinued, whether
from the artifices of Illuminati bookſellers,
to prevent its ſale and ſpread, or from the author's bad health, I know not."

In a ſubſequent letter, of June 13, 1801,
ſpeaking of the forementioned criminations
of Dr. Robiſon's character, which have been

circulated in America, the Dr. fays, " Had
they been fent to Edinburgh, for their PALPA-
BLE FALSEHOOD, they would have been *deſpiſ-
ed* and *deteſted.*"

In the appendix to the Centurial Sermon of
Dr. Dwight, Prefident of Yale College, publifhed Jan. 7, 1801, is an atteftation to the
character of Profeffor Robifon, taken from
a letter of Mr. J. Walker, a refpectable inhab-
itant of Great Britain, to Profeffor Boëttiger,
of Weimar in Germany ; publifhed in the
Mercury of that city, April, 1800. " It was
written in anfwer to fome very fevere afperfions on Mr. Robifon, by Mr. Boëttiger ; and
fuch was the character of the writer, and
fuch the weight of his teftimony, that Mr.
Boëttiger amply, as well as honorably, re-
tracted his afperfions." Referring to the exalted character he had given of Dr. Robifon,
he fays, " Nor is this the exaggerated praife
of a friend ; no one who knows Mr. Robifon, as I have known him, and he is almoſt
univerfally known in Britain, will dare to
call it in queftion."*

* I have further evidence on this fubject, but I conceive it needlefs to introduce it. What is laid before the
reader is more than fufficient to eftablifh Dr. Robifon's
character. It adds no fmall weight to his opinion ; and

The character of the Abbe Barruel, so far as it respects his credibility as a witness, I believe has not been impeached. The honest warmth, apparent in every part of his celebrated work, renders it difficult for us to doubt his sincerity, whatever opinion we may form of his judgment. If the fervor of his zeal has hurried him into a rash censure, or an unwarrantable conclusion, does not the same fervor compel us to respect him as a writer, who felt the truth and importance of his subject? Shall we condemn him because he writes with the ardor of the most exquisite feelings? How could he but feel, when he saw the religion and government which he loved, demolished, and the country, above all others dear to him, converted into a field of carnage, and bleeding at every pore, pierced with the daggers of men, who " owed their greatness to their country's ruin?" His attachment to principles not admitted in America, has doubtless weakened the impressions which his testimony ought to have

affords us a degree of assurance, that what he has published upon the subject of Illuminism, is neither visionary nor trifling. The reputation he had acquired in the literary world, forbids us to suppose that he would have added his name to such a publication, unless convinced that the facts he states, and attests, were important and well authenticated.

made. While we hear him pleading in support of sentiments in religion, which in our view are absurd ; advocating a government, which we consider as tyrannical; and denouncing societies as dangerous, of which we ourselves, perhaps, are innocent members, we naturally connect the absurdity of these sentiments, with the facts adduced in their support. It is an obvious remark, that the value of these Memoirs consists, not in the religious or political opinions, but in the important facts, they contain. These appear, generally, to be stated with great accuracy, and with a strict regard to truth ; and from these, the author candidly invites us to judge for ourselves. As became an honest man, together with his opinion, he has given us the facts and circumstances upon which that opinion was founded ; leaving the reader to correct, if he see cause, his too hasty judgment.

That the Abbe, by making his own sentiments the standard in politics and religion, has censured some persons whom protestants and republicans would justify, is not to be denied ; but has he asserted any thing as a fact, without stating carefully the evidence upon which his opinion was founded ?

It is obvious that the testimony of these
writers is greatly strengthened by its remarkable coincidence. It appears that Dr. Robison's work was published just as the third
volume of the Abbe's Memoirs was going to
the press, and precisely in those circumstances,
which must have prevented either of them
from suggesting to the other, either the plan
of their proposed publications, or the principal authorities by which they are authenticated. The remarkable difference which appears in these two writers with respect to
their methods of arranging, and communicating their thoughts; their very different
ideas of religious and political truth; the obscurity which, from the nature of it, attended the subject; the many remote circumstances with which it was connected, and es-
pecially the different plans they pursue; Dr.
Robison combining, in one paragraph, what
his memory compiled from many, while the
Abbe, as he declares, " never made a quotation but with the original before him; and
when," says he, " I make a translation which
may stagger the reader, I subjoin the original,
that each may explain and verify the text;"
these things taken into view, a greater degree
of harmony could not be expected from any

two hiftorians relating events of equal magnitude.*

But we have to encounter ftill more formidable oppofition than any which has yet
appeared, and that is Profeffor Ebeling's
letter to his correfpondent in Maffachu-
fetts, and publifhed in the Worcefter Gazette, October 9, 1799. This letter appears
to have been confidered, by fome, as containing plenary evidence againft the veracity of
Dr. Robifon, and the credibility of his book.
But, had not this letter been read with the
fame hafte and eagernefs with which it appears to have been written, certainly fo much
importance would not have been attached
to it.

---

* The following teftimony, in favor of the authenticity
of the works in queftion, is from a late refpectable writer.

" The rife and progrefs of Jacobinifm, which feems
to include every fpecies of Infidelity, have been examined with induftry, and difplayed with correctnefs, by
the Abbe Barruel and Profeffor Robifon. The facts
brought forward in fupport of their affertions, have baf-
fled the ingenuity of Jacobinifm itfelf to difprove. And
thefe facts have clearly fhown, that a *confpiracy* was actually formed for the extinction of Chriftianity, and the
abolition of government and focial order, by a fet of
men whofe names demand the execration of mankind."
Kett, on Prophecy, Lond. edition, 1800, Vol. II, p. 119.

Upon reading this letter we naturally recollect an obfervation made by Profeffor Renner, one of the witneffes from whom the public received the firft difclofure of the Illuminated focieties. " There are men ;" fays he, " who defend the order with great warmth, though they do not declare themfelves to belong to it. Such conduct certainly deferves a little animadverfion. Either thefe defenders belong to the order, or they do not ; if they do not, can they pretend to defend that which they neither know, nor have any poffibility of knowing ? If they belong to the order, that very circumftance renders them unworthy of belief."* The propriety of this remark will imprefs the reader more forcibly, when he is better acquainted with the arts by which the Illuminees conceal themfelves from the public.

The great ftrefs which has been laid upon this letter, and the ufe which has been made of it, will juftify our beftowing on it particular attention.

It may be of fome importance to recollect, that Mr. Ebeling has acknowledged that it

---

* Barruel's Memoirs, Vol. IV. p. 149.

was written in hafte, and was, confequently, inaccurate. It was unfortunate that this information was not communicated, as ufual, at the clofe of the letter, where it might have been ufeful to guard us againft placing too much dependence on a hafty and inaccurate performance ; but it was given in a fubfequent letter, after being informed that the previous one had been made public. Though this apology came too late for us, it may be ufeful to the Profeffor, and afford him a retreat, fhould fome of his many confident declarations, hereafter appear to be founded in error.

Mr. Ebeling confiders Dr. Robifon's mifreprefentations, as the refult of wicked intention ; fpeaks of him as " an *Englifh hired, minifterial writer ;*" and tells us, " his book is certainly a party work, and not without a *political defign.*" In another part of the fame letter he afcribes Robifon's mifreprefentations to his "*great ignorance of men, manners, and hiftory, and of German characters, and language* in particular." Perhaps Mr. Ebeling can reconcile thefe two contradictory caufes of the fame effect. The talk is beyond my ability. From thefe very different reprefentations, I can obtain no idea but this abfurd one, that Dr.

Robison was hired by the British miniſtry, to give ſuch a wrong view of things as would ſerve their political purpoſes ; that he undertook the taſk, and by the luckieſt miſtake ſtumbled upon that very ſpot at which he was aiming, and which, had it not been for his groſs ignorance of men, manners, and hiſtory, of German characters, and language, he probably never would have attained. Let this form a new item among the advantages of ignorance.

But we have more important remarks to make upon this celebrated letter. Mr. Ebeling ſpeaks of the exiſtence of Illuminiſm in Germany, as a matter of public notoriety ; but, to preſerve the impreſſion of its harmleſs nature, he ſays of the Illuminees, " their deſign was undoubtedly to prevent political and religious oppreſſion ;" and with a particular reference to Weiſhaupt, the grand projector of Illuminiſm, further adds, " he was, as I ſuppoſe commonly Roman Catholics are, when they ſee the errors of ſuperſtition, and know nothing of the proteſtant faith, or true religion, *at a loſs what to ſubſtitute.*" Weiſhaupt then, it is confeſſed, wiſhed to deſtroy the beſt religion he was acquainted with. He conſidered popery as the religion of the Bible, and

this was hateful fuperstition. It appears, therefore, from this statement of his Apologist,
that he would have spared no religion, for in
his view there was no fubstitute for popery.
The reader will obferve, that Weishaupt was a
Professor in an University, and distinguished
for his literary acquirements : that he had
framed many new fystems of Christianity. to
deceive his adepts ; that Germany abounded
with proteftants of every denomination, but
still there was no religion to his taste, no fubftitute for popery.

Mr. Ebeling also acknowledges that Weishaupt, " in his younger life, was guilty of *great
deviations from pure morality,*" but in the fame
paragraph in which he gives us this view of
his moral character, and in the fame paragraph
in which he acknowledges, that Weishaupt
could find no religion in all Germany, nor in
the Bible, better than popery, which he hated,
and was endeavoring to overturn ; Mr. Ebeling difplays his invincible charity by adding,
" but I am not convinced that he (Weishaupt)
was *ever in theory, or practice, an enemy to religion ! !*" Left the reader fhould not extend that
charity to Mr. Ebeling, of which he himfelf is
fo liberal, it may be neceffary here to remind
him, that the Profeffor wrote in hafte. In the

confufion of his thoughts he muft have loft
the impreffion which Weifhaupt's character had
formerly made upon his mind, and in the hur-
ry of the moment, he marked the *infidel and
the debauchee, for a chriftian ;* for nothing lefs
can he be who never was, " either in theory
or practice, an enemy to religion."

One great difadvantage, indeed, refults from
this exuberance of the Profeffor's hafty charity, for who can affure us, that he has not
equally miftaken the many other characters,
he introduces into his letter ? This confideration muft diminifh that fund of correct information, which fome imagine they poffefs in
this long epiftle, and leave us room to doubt,
at leaft, whether Dr. Robifon *was fo very ignorant* of men and manners as he is reprefented.

But will not this letter affift us in attaining
fomething beyond probabilities and conjecture ? Mr. Ebeling has faid much to difcredit
the other authorities to which Dr. Robifon
occafionally recurs for proof ; but I find nothing to weaken the evidence refulting from the
teftimony of the four very refpectable witneffes, given under oath, refpecting the practices
of the Illuminees ; nor, as far as I am able to
afcertain, does he exprefs a doubt refpecting

the writings, letters, and documents, found in the hands of the Society on the fearch made in confequence of the teftimony abovementioned. Here we have the code of the Society, their private correfpondence, and their own remarks upon the nature and defign of the inftitution ; thefe are admitted to be genuine ; and on thefe, as their proper bafis, Robifon and Barruel raife their fuperftructure. Have we not here a clue, which will lead us out of this labyrinth of difcordant opinions ? Let us examine carefully, the ground on which we ftand.

It is agreed, that a Society of Illuminees exifted in Germany, inftituted by Weifhaupt, about the year 1776. It is agreed, that the papers found in the pofleffion of Counfellor Zwack, in 1786, and thofe found in the Caftle of Sanderdorf, in 1787, on fearch made by order of his Highnefs the Elector of Bavaria, are authentic documents, drawn up by the Illuminees, expreffing the plan and object of the order. It is agreed, that the object of this inftitution is the overthrow of all religion, and all government. No ;—this, though ftrangely afferted by Meffrs. Robifon and Barruel, Mr. Ebeling denies. To determine on which fide the truth lies, we muft appeal to the pa-

C

pers which are admitted to be authentic, and
from them judge for ourfelves what were the
real views of the Illuminees. By attacking
every other witnefs in the caufe, Mr. Ebeling,
by his filence, concerning the papers, has implicitly acknowledged their truth and validity.

The reader is here reminded, that the queftion to be determined is not, whether Illuminifm had an exiftence ; this is admitted :
Nor whether it exifted as an organized body,
poffefling its code of laws, and definite mode
of operation ; for Mr. Ebeling himfelf informs
us, that the Illuminees were inftituted, or
formed into a body, about 1776. Nor is it a
queftion whether this order of men had any
thing in view beyond their own amufement,
for the fame advocate of their caufe obferves,
" that their defign undoubtedly was, to prevent political and religious oppreffion." But
the important queftion to be determined is,
whether this combination of men had not a
higher object ? whether their ultimate aim
was not the fubverfion of every focial, moral,
and religious obligation ? Taking this for our
object, it will be needlefs to introduce into
this work that part of the evidence above referred to, which relates particularly to the fubverfion of the Romifh hierarchy and defpot-

ifm, or political and religious oppreflion ; for all acknowledge that thefe were aimed at by the confpiracy. Our prefent concern is, with that part only of thefe writings which relates to the principal queftion, and is calculated to prove, that the Illuminees were oppofed to the fundamental principles of all religion, and fo-cial order.

The Abbe Barruel's Memoirs comprehend a larger period of time than Dr. Robifon's work ; his arrangements are more fyftemat-ical, and he traces the evil to its fource ; his method, without, however, being confined to it, will be principally followed.

The Abbe Barruel's plan includes,

Firft. The *Anti-chriftian Confpiracy*, or that of the Sophifters of impiety againft Chriftiani-ty, under every form and denomination.

Secondly. The *Anti-Monarchical Confpiracy*. This part will be omitted in the following work, as unconnected with the queftion in view, and becaufe it is involved in the

Third, or *Anti-Social Confpiracy*, in which the fophifters of impiety, coalefce with the fophifters of Anarchy againft every religion, and every government, under the denomination of *Illuminees ;* and, *theſe* again unite themſelves with the occult Lodges of Free Maſons, and thus form the club of the *Jacobins* at Paris, who are the real directors of the French Revolution. This *third part* embraces the ſubject of the Conſpiracy of which Dr. Robiſon treats ; and is more particularly in⸗ tereſting in our preſent inquiry.

The *evidence* adduced in proof of the *Anti-Chriſtian Conſpiracy,* are the writings of the Conſpirators themſelves ; eſpecially the Edition of Voltaire's Works, by Beaumarchis. Theſe Works, it appears, were publiſhed when the ſentiments they contain, were no longer conſidered as infamous in France.*

* The proofs of the Anti-Social Conſpiracy will be noticed in connection with that part of the ſubject to which they relate. The reader will not expect to find, in this work, the particular references of the larger work, tranſcribed ; except where ſome authority, not before mentioned, is introduced. This would be needleſs, as the few, who would wiſh to recur to the original authorities, may find every neceſſary reference in the tranſlation of Barruel's Memoirs, printed at Hartford, by Hudſon and Goodwin, 1799; and in the fourth Edition of Robiſon's Proofs, &c. printed at New-York, by George Forman, in 1799 ; which are the Editions made uſe of in forming this abſtract.

The Author of thefe Memoirs declares it to be the important and friendly defign of his undertaking, to warn governments and mankind of their danger, by proving to them, that the French Revolution, in all the circumftances of horror which attended it, was the natural refult of the principles from which it proceeded ; and that *fimilar principles will produce fimilar effects.* Left any, confiding in their leagues of amity with France, and her profeffions of friendfhip, fhould imagine the warning needlefs with refpect to themfelves, he again founds the alarm. Let America hear !

" When the phantom of peace fhall feem to terminate the prefent war, between the Jacobins and the combined powers, it certainly will be the intereft of all governments to afcertain how far fuch a peace can be relied on. At that period, more than any other, will it be neceffary to ftudy the fecret hiftory of that fect ; at that period we muft remember, that it is not in the field of Mars that the war againft fects is the moft dangerous ; that is a war of plots and confpiracies, and againft them public treaties can never avail."*

* ...., Barruel's Memoirs, Vol. I.

C H A P. I.

The Actors, Existence, Object, and Secret of the Conspiracy.

PHENOMENA of the moſt aſtoniſhing nature have, within a few years paſt, arreſted the attention of mankind. Manners, and the ſtate of ſociety, have undergone a revolution which has appeared to extinguiſh, in many, every natural affection, and to transform the moſt civilized and poliſhed, into the moſt ferocious of men. The beſt eſtabliſhed principles of natural and revealed religion, and the very foundations of moral and ſocial duty, obligations never before controverted, have been attacked by an hoſt of enemies. A flood of infidelity has deluged the greater part of the Chriſtianized world, threatening to ſweep away every veſtige of Chriſtianity. And may it not be ſaid, almoſt without a metaphor, that by an horrid Anti-Chriſtian regeneration, a nation of Atheiſts have been born in a day?

Thefe are plain facts ; and they demand the moft ferious attention of mankind. It is not by framing fanciful theories, but by carefully tracing effects to their caufes, that we acquire ufeful knowledge and experience. Some ad-equate caufe, there muft have been, of this mighty mifchief. Whence fhall we date its origin ? To what fhall we afcribe its rife and progrefs ? In anfwer to thefe queries we pre-fume to fay, that however acceffary other caufes may have been, the principal caufe is to be found in the following hiftorical abftract.

About the middle of the laft century there appeared three men, leagued in the moft in-veterate hatred againft Chriftianity, VOLTAIRE the Chief, D'ALEMBERT, diftinguifhed for his fubtilty, and FREDERIC II. King of Pruffia ; to which number was afterwards added DI-DEROT, whom, probably on account of his frantic impiety, the hiftorian characterifes, the *forlorn hope.*

The neceffary brevity of this work will not permit us to defcend to a particular view of their feveral characters, yet the firft of thefe confpirators is fo diftinguifhed in this work, and in the literary world, as to juftify a more particular attention.

Voltaire, the son of an ancient notary of the Chatelet, was born at Paris, February 20, 1694. His original name was Mary Francis Arouet, which, through vanity, he changed to Voltaire, as more sonorous, and more conformable to the reputation at which he aimed. He was eminently distinguished for his abilities, and for his thirst of dominion over the literary world. His talents, however, were more brilliant than solid, less fitted for deep investigation, but eminently calculated to amuse and captivate. He possessed all those passions which render abilities dangerous; and, unhappily, his appeared to be all early devoted to the overthrow of religion. While a student, he received the following prophetic rebuke from his Professor: " Unfortunate young man, you will one day come to be the standard bearer of infidelity."*

After leaving the College he associated with men of abandoned morals; and having given offence to the French government by some satirical essays, he sought an asylum in England. There he first conceived the design of overthrowing religion by *blending Philosophy with Impiety*. Condorcet, his adept, his confident,

* Life of Voltaire, Lib. of Ecl.

his hiftorian, and panegyrift, afferts in pofitive terms, " *There it was that Voltaire fwore to dedicate his life to the accomplifhment of that project ; and he has kept his word.*"*

On his return to Paris, about the year 1730, he became fo open in his defigns, and fo fanguine in his hopes, that Mr. Herault, the lieutenant of Police, remarked to him, " *You may do or write what you pleafe, you will never be able to deftroy the Chriftian religion.*" Voltaire, without hefitation, anfwered, " *That is what we fhall fee.*"†

While he yet flattered himfelf with the hopes of enjoying, alone, the whole glory of deftroying the Chriftian religion, (though he foon found that affociates would be neceffary) " *I am weary,*" he would fay, " *of hearing people repeat, that twelve men have been fufficient to eftablifh Chriftianity, and I will prove that one may fuffice to overthrow it.*"‡

Frederic alfo, dignified among the fophifters, with the title of " the Solomon of the North," and by the hiftorian with the epithet of " The Great," claims, even in this brief

* Life of Voltaire, Edit. of Kell. † Ibid. ‡ Ibid.

sketch, a more particular notice. To express his contrary, and almost irreconcileable qualities, we find him painted a double man, exhibiting two distinct and opposite characters. In one view of him, we see the hero, and the father of his people, giving life to agriculture and commerce ; in another, the sophister, the philosophical pedant, the conspirator against Christianity. The contradictions in his character are transcribed in his letters ; at one time, extolling, in glowing terms, the morality of the gospel ; and at another, asserting, that " *Christianity yields none but poisonous weeds.*"

There can be no doubt, however, that Frederic united cordially, as he did early, with the enemies of religion. Even at that early age, when he was only Prince-Royal, in his correspondence with Voltaire, he had adopted the style of the modern Philosopher ; for he thus writes, " To speak with my usual freedom, I must naturally own, that whatever regards the *God made man*, displeases me in the mouth of a Philosopher, who should be above popular error. We may speak of fables, but merely as fables ; and a profound silence, in my opinion, should be kept, concerning those fables of the

Chriftians, fanctified by time and the credulity of the abfurd and ftupid."*

But what did this boafted wifdom avail? While foaring, in imagination, far above their fellow mortals, we fee them in the fame fituation in which every perfon will find him-felf, who relinquifhes the guiding light of Revelation, wandering in the wildernefs with-out a path, and without a compafs. " Is there a God fuch as he is faid to be ? A foul fuch as is imagined ? Is there any thing to be hoped for after this life ?" Thefe queftions, the *com-fortable* fruits of infidelity, were propofed by Voltaire to D'Alembert ; to which he anfwers, with the fame *admirable* philofophic wifdom, that " *No*, in metaphyfics, appeared to him not much wifer than *yes ;* and that *non liquet* (it is not clear) was generally the only rational

* As Frederic is another of Mr. Ebeling's Chriftians, who, he intimates, died in the hope of a better life, I beg leave to introduce a fhort fketch of his character, drawn by a fkilful, and apparently, impartial pen. " Moft unjuft-ly (fays the writer) is he ftyled *great ;* a philofophical monarch, the moft defpotic, perhaps, who ever exifted, but who has contributed more to the diffolution of fociety, by corrupting the principles and morals of all within the fphere of his influence, than any individual of his time. See Appendix to Vol. 6, of Anti-Jacobin Review, p. 565.

anfwer."* Who would not give up the Bible
for the honor and comfort of being fo nobly
and philofophically bewildered?

Senfible that the individual infidelity of
thefe perfons did not conftitute a confpiracy
againft Chriftianity, without a union and correfpondence in the attack, the hiftorian has
furnifhed us with the proofs of fuch a confederacy, in which their efforts, and thofe of their
adepts, appear combined and fteadily pointed
to the accomplifhment of their grand object.
To this object they directed and ftimulated
each other by a watchword, ftrikingly expreffive of their rancorous enmity to the Saviour,
ecrafez l' infame ! crufh the wretch. But could
this mean Chrift, and that adorable religion
preached by him and his apoftles? What other
interpretation can we annex to the phrafe in
the mouth of a man, who, in his intrigues
againft " the wretch," exclaims, " Could not
five or fix men of parts, and who rightly underftood each other, fucceed, after the examples of *twelve fcoundrels,* who have already fucceeded?" And who thus writes to D'Alembert,
" Both you and Demilaville muft be well
pleafed, to fee the contempt into which " the

* Barruel's Memoirs, Vol. I. Chap. 1.

wretch" is fallen among the better fort of
people throughout Europe. They were all
we wifhed for, or that were neceffary. We
never pretended to enlighten the houfe maids,
and fhoe makers ; we leave them to the apoftles."* The apoftles furely were neither Jefuits nor Janfenifts ; their only crime, in Voltaire's view, doubtlefs was, attachment to their
mafter and his caufe.

In the true ftyle of confpirators, they had
alfo their enigmatical language, and fecret appropriate names. The general term for the
confpirators was *Cacouac ;* they fay one is a
good Cacouac, when he can be perfectly depended on. In their correfpondence, Frederic
is called Duluc ; Voltaire, Raton ; D'Alembert, Protagoras and Bertrand ; Diderot, Pla-
to or Tamplot. Secrecy appears to have been
confidered by them as effential to their fuccefs.
Their Chief would therefore often remind
them that in the war they waged, " they were
to act as confpirators, and not as zealots.
Strike," he would fay, " hurl the Javelin, but
hide your hand."

D

* Barruel's Memoirs, Vol. I. Chap. 2.

Voltaire had long before vented his rage against Christianity, and been the officious defender of every impious publication ; but, about 1752, when he returned from Berlin, the conspiracy assumed a regular form, and he, by his age, reputation, and genius, naturally became the chief.*

* Barruel's Memoirs, Vol. I. Chap. 3.

C H A P. II.

The Means of the Conspirators.

ESTABLISHED in the general proceſs of undermining the Chriſtian Edifice, and thus obliging it to fall of itſelf, as one powerful mean of effecting this end, an Encyclopedia was projected by D'Alembert, and announced to the world, as a complete treaſure of all human arts and ſciences, but which, in reality, was deſigned to be the emporium of all the ſophiſms and calumnies which had ever been invented againſt religion. This poiſon, however, was to be conveyed in the moſt ſecret and unſuſpicious manner, and it was declared, that all the religious articles ſhould be compiled by learned and orthodox divines. Particular care was taken in the compilation of the firſt volume, not to alarm the friends of religion ; reſerving a clearer expreſſion of their ſentiments for ſucceeding volumes.

Among the many artful means adopted to
communicate the fecret infection, one was, to
infinuate error and infidelity, not where it
would have been expected, but into thofe articles deemed the leaft fufceptible of them ; fuch
as Hiftory, Natural Philofophy, and Chym-
iftry.*

Another was that of references, by which,
after being prefented with fome religious
truths, the reader is invited to feek further
information in articles of a different caft.
Sometimes the reference would direct to an
epigram, or farcafm. After having treated a
religious fubject with all poffible refpect, it
would be fimply added, See the article *Prejudice*, or *Superftition*, or *Fanaticifm*.†

The following may ferve as a fpecimen of
the artful ufe of references, in this work, for

---

* Mr. Paley, in his Syftem of Moral Philofophy, has
noticed, and very juftly defcribed, the fubtle arts of modern
impiety. " Infidelity is now ferved up in every fhape that
is likely to allure, furprife or beguile the imagination ; in
a fable, a tale, a novel, a poem, in interfperfed and broken
hints ; remote and oblique furmifes ; in books of travels,
of philofophy, of natural hiftory ; in a word, in any form
rather than that of a profeffed and regular difquifition. "
Paley, Bofton Edit. 1795, p. 302.

† Barruel's Memoirs, Vol. I. Chap. 4.

undermining religious truth. Under the article GOD, you find found fentiments, together with a direct and complete proof of his exiftence. From this the reader is referred to the article *Demonftration.* There all direct demonftrations of the exiftence of God difappear ; and we are told, that a fingle infect more forcibly proves the being of a God, than any other arguments whatever. But the reader is ftill referred to the article *Corruption.* There it is afferted, that daily experiments feem to prove, that " corruption may produce animated bodies." The reader is thus left to infer, if he pleafes, that the ftrongeft proof of the exiftence of a God is contradicted by daily experiments.

Notwithftanding all this art and concealment, the work met with great oppofition, and was for a time fufpended. At length, however, it was completed, and all the adepts were loud in its praifes. The learned were duped. The work fold. Various editions were publifhed, and under the pretence of correcting, each fucceeding edition was more highly charged with infidelity.*

D 2

* Barruel's Memoirs, Vol. I. Chap. 4. Note.

The Encyclopedia having prepared the way, was succeeded by an attempt to overturn the religious orders. This ended in the suppression of many of them, and in the expulsion of the Jesuits, in 1764. The artful movements, by which this was effected, are not sufficiently interesting to claim a particular detail. Some, who appear to have been friendly to the Romish establishment, but not sufficiently considering the connection between a church and its clergy, were drawn by these sophisters to countenance, and even promote the suppression of the religious orders ; and we see these conspirators ridiculing, in secret, the simplicity of their dupes.*

Mankind were extremely deceived by the insincere professions of the conspirators. Nothing, perhaps, contributed more to their success than their pretensions to *toleration*, *reason*, and *humanity*. But notwithstanding these high sounding words, their secret correspondence betrays the same spirit which has since been exhibited in the revolution. Was it *humanity* which dictated to Voltaire his wish, " to see every Jesuit at the bottom of the ocean, with a Jansenist at his neck ?' He was much engaged to deprive the ecclesiastical princes of

* Barruel's Memoirs, Vol. I. Chap. 5, 6.

their poffeflions, and the clergy of their means
of fupport ; and exerted his influence, with
Frederic, and the Duke of Praflin in particular, for this end. Writing to Count Argental
upon this fubject, he fays, " Had I but an hundred thoufand men, I well know what I would
do with them." Would he then preach toleration and humanity ? We may judge from his
own expreflions what his views were. " It is
noble, he writes to Frederic, to fcoff at thefe
Harlequin Bull-givers. I like to cover them
with ridicule, *but I had rather plunder them.*"*

Proteftants will perhaps confider the fuppref-
fion of thefe orders as having no connection
with the interefts of religion ; but they were
the great props of this caufe as it exifted
in France ; were active in withftanding the
progrefs of infidelity, and their overthrow was
undoubtedly, as it was viewed by thefe confpirators, of great importance to the comple-
tion of their ultimate defign ; the eftablifhment
of univerfal infidelity.

Wearied with the oppofition he met with in
France, and the eonftant conftraint to which he
was fubjected, Voltaire projected the eftablifh-

* Barruel's Memoirs, Vol. I. Chap. 10.

ment of a colony of Philofophers, at Cleves,
under the jurifdiction of Frederic, who might
there, as he expreffes his views, "freely and bold-
ly fpeak the truth, without fearing minifters,
priefts, or parliaments." But this, though a
favorite object with the projector, proved
abortive. The confpirators were too much
captivated with the pleafures of Paris, and the
applaufe they found in the circles of their admirers, to be fond of fuch a retirement ; and
leaft of all, was it eligible, in company with
Voltaire, whofe more fplendid genius would
eclipfe his fatellites."*

But a more important attempt, met with
different fucccefs. The higheft literary hon-
or in France was a feat in the French Academy. This inftitution, defigned to be both
a ftimulus, and reward to literary merit, had
enjoyed the fpecial favor and protection of the
kings of France ; and none but men of emi-
nence in fome branch of literature, and who
were viewed as friendly to morals and religion, had been admitted as members. The
artful D'Alembert concealed his infidelity until he had gained his feat. Voltaire was for
a long time unable to gain admiffion, and

* Barruel's Memoirs, Vol. I. Chap. 7.

at length only fucceeded by means of high
protection, and that low hypocrify which
he recommended to his difciples.

The confpirators juftly eftimated the advantages which would refult to their grand
object, by removing the difqualifying bar of
infidelity, and annexing to philofophifm the
refpectability and influence of fuch an inftitution. Upon Voltaire and D'Alembert lay the
tafk, of converting thefe dignified feats of
fcience into the haunts of Atheifm. We may
judge of their fuccefs, from the following anecdote. Mr. Beauzet, a member of the academy, refpectable for his piety, when afked
how he could ever have been affociated with
fuch notorious unbelievers ? " The very fame
queftion," faid he, " I put to D'Alembert. At
one of the fittings, feeing that *I was nearly the
only perfon who believed in God,* I afked him, how
he poffibly could ever have thought of me for
a member, when he knew that my fentiments
and opinions differed fo widely from thofe of
his brethren ? D'Alembert, without hefitation,
anfwered, " We were in want of a fkilful
grammarian, and among our party, not one
had made himfelf a reputation in that line."
It is almoft needlefs to remark, that the rewards of literary merit were henceforth tranf-

ferred to the advocates of impiety, while reproach and infamy were profufely caft upon
thofe who efpoufed the caufe of truth.*

Their fuccefs in fecuring the Academy to
themfelves, prepared the way for that variety
of Anti-Chriftian writings, which of late have
been fo widely diffeminated, and which have
been pointed againft religion.   Aftonifhing
efforts were made to weaken the evidences of
the Chriftian hiftory.   The furface of the
earth underwent a new furvey, and its bowels
were explored, not to promote the interefts of
literature, which was the oftenfible object, nor
to obtain the pious pleafure which the good
man feels in contemplating the works of the
Creator ; but,

> ————" Some drill and bore
> The folid earth, and from the ftrata there
> Extract a regifter, by which we learn
> That he who made it and reveal'd its date
> To Mofes, was miftaken in its age."

Yet then, as now, they who were alarmed by
thefe Anti-Chriftian theories, and gave warning of the danger, were held up to the public
as weakly timid, " For what," it was impu-

dently afked, " have philofophical treatifes to
do with religion ?"

But while Voltaire faw the expediency, of
what he calls, " *fome ferious work*," fome publication which fhould have the femblance of
reafon and philofophy, the weapon on which
he principally depended, was ridicule. Deifts
have long found this their beft mode of attack ; but the genius of Voltaire was peculiarly fruitful in anecdotes, jefts, and farcafms.
" I only afk," he writes to D'Alembert, " five
or fix witticifms a day, that would fuffice.
It (meaning " the wretch") would not get
the better of them. Laugh Democritus, make
me laugh, and the fages fhall carry the day."

But not content with engroffing literary honors, the confpirators condefcended, at length,
to enlighten thofe whom they had contemptuoufly called the houfe maids and fhoe makers.
Writings, in every form and fhape, calculated
to excite licentious defires, to deprave the
moral tafte, to communicate the infection of
infidelity, and exhibit religion in a ridiculous
view, were crowded upon the public.

Upon the commencement of the revolution,
it appeared, by the confeffion of Le Roy, who

had been their fecretary, that a fociety, which
had exifted for a confiderable time, holding
their meetings at the Hotel de Holbach, at
Paris, under the name of Economifts, was
compofed of thefe confpirators and their principal adepts ; and who, while profeffedly engaged in promoting economy, agriculture, and
the ufeful arts, were more actively promoting
the caufe of infidelity. A multitude of writers were employed to prepare fuitable publications. Thefe, previous to their going to the
prefs, were fubjected to the infpection of the
fociety, whofe care it was to charge them with
a due proportion of the poifonous leaven
they were defigned to diffeminate. To add
refpectability to thefe writings, and conceal
the author, the fociety appointed under what
title they fhould be publifhed. For inftance,
" *Chriftianity Unveiled*," was attributed to Bou-
langer, after his death, but was the work of
Demilaville.

Elegant editions of thefe works were firft
printed to defray the expenfe, and then an im-
menfe number on the pooreft paper. Thefe
latter, were diftributed in bales, free of coft, or
at a very low price, to hawkers and pedlars,
who would difperfe them through the country, and left any fhould efcape the infection,

clubs were formed, and perfons hired to read them to fuch as were unable to read.

Mr. Bertin, one of the French miniftry, declares, that in his excurfions into the country, he found the pedlars loaded with the writings of Voltaire, Diderot, and other philofophifts ; and that, queftioning them how the country people could find money for fuch dear works, their conftant anfwer was, " We have them at a much cheaper rate than *Prayer Books ;* we may fell them at ten fols (5*d.*) a volume, and have a pretty profit into the bargain ; and many of them owned that thefe books coft them nothing."

But the queftion in which we are principally interefted is, whether it was the defign of thefe numerous publications to affect any thing more than that deformed excrefcence of Chriftianity, popery ? If it has not been made evident that thefe writings were aimed, not at the abufes of Chriftianity, but at Chriftianity itfelf, a view of the leading fentiments in thefe publications, muft remove every doubt.

Freret tells us exprefsly, that, " The God of the Jews, and of the Chriftians, is but a phantom and chimera ;" and that, " all ideas of

E

justice and injustice, of virtue and vice, are arbitrary, and dependent on custom."

The author of " *Good Sense*," a work which D'Alembert wished to see abridged, that it might be sold for *five pence* to the poor and ignorant, teaches, " That the wonders of nature, so far from bespeaking a God, are but the neceſſary effects of matter, prodigiouſly diverſified, and that the soul is a chimera."

The author of the " *Doubts*" tells mankind, " That they cannot know whether a God really exists, or whether there exists the smallest difference between virtue and vice."

Helvetius informs the fair ſex, " That modeſty is only an invention of refined voluptuouſneſs." He teaches children, " That the commandment of loving their parents, is more the work of education than nature ;" and the married couple, " That the law which condemns to live together, becomes barbarous and cruel on the day they ceaſe to love each other."

The author of " *Chriſtianity Unveiled*," has this remark, " The Bible ſays, the fear of the Lord is the beginning of wiſdom. I think it rather the beginning of folly."

But I shall only add to this detail, *John Mef-lier's laft will,* in which he is reprefented " on his death bed, imploring forgivenefs of his God for having taught Chriftianity ;" a work, of which Voltaire urges D'Alembert to print and diftribute four or five thoufand copies ; complaining " that there were not fo many in all Paris, as he himfelf had diftributed throughout the mountains of Switzerland."*

The confpirators appear to have been aware of the importance of youth, and the advantage to be derived to their caufe, by an early impreffion on the young mind. D'Alembert, lefs qualified to promote the views of the confpirators by his pen, attended more particularly to providing inftructors. Care was taken that he fhould receive early notice of vacant profefforfhips in colleges, and of vacant fchools, that they might be filled agreeably to their wifhes. It will be readily conceived that pupils of rank, wealth, and talents, would engage fpecial attention. D'Alembert was the open protector of all fuch, who vifited Paris. The extenfive correfpondence of Voltaire, and the eclat of his genius, gave him a vaft opportunity of infecting youth, even in foreign courts.

* Barruel's Memoirs, Vol. I. Chap. 9, 17; and Note.

At that time the court of Parma was seeking men worthy to preside over the education
of the young infant. The account which Voltaire gave of the result of that business, will
abundantly explain the views of the conspirators in this point. Writing to D'Alembert,
he says, " It appears to me that the Parmesan
child will be well surrounded. He will have
a Condillac and a de Leire. *If with all that he
is a bigot, grace must be powerful indeed.*"*

Among the innumerable attempts of these
ever plotting philosophists, the following curious instance of zeal is related of Diderot and
D'Alembert. They frequently met in the
coffee houses at Paris, to discuss religious questions, before the idle Parisians. In these dif-
putes Diderot would appear in his proper
character of an infidel, D'Alembert assuming
that of an advocate for religion ; and apparently espousing its cause with great warmth,
until driven by the victorious infidel from every ground of defence, he would retreat, to
appearance chagrined, and regretting that his
religion afforded no better arguments for its
defence. The impression which such a scene
must leave upon the minds of those present,

* Barruel's Memoirs, Vol. I. Chap. 11.

who were ignorant of the deception, need not be told.*

Their defire to " *crufb the wretch*," fuggeft-ed alfo to thefe confpirators the idea of re-building the temple at Jerufalem, with a view of defeating the predictions of Chrift, and the prophet Daniel. This had been long fince at-tempted by Julian the apoftate, with the fame defign, when flames and balls of fire burfting from the foundations, and repeatedly deftroy-ing the workmen, compelled him to defift from his purpofe.† This rendered D'Alem-bert and Voltaire more defirous of depriving Scripture prophecy of fuch a glorious attefta-tion to its truth. With this view, application was made both to Frederic and the Emprefs of Ruffia, to engage them to ufe their influ-

E 2

* Barruel's Memoirs, Vol. I. Chap. 11.

† This miracle is recorded by many witneffes, and more particularly by Ammianus Marcellinus, a pagan author, and friend of Julian. The truth of this miracle is denied, indeed, by Bafnage ; but its authenticity appears to be fully eftablifhed in a learned differtation upon the fubject, by Dr. Warburton, in which the objections of Bafnage are particularly examined, and refuted.

ence with the Turkish powers, to whose ju-
risdiction Jerusalem pertained, to promote
the design ; but the fear of losing many
wealthy Jews, whom they found profitable
subjects, and who, in that case, would have
repaired to their new temple, prevented the
attempt.*

To reconcile many things, of a very different
aspect in the conduct and writings of these
men, with the purposes here attributed to
them, it is necessary the reader should be informed, that all these designs were industriously concealed under a covert of hypocrisy.
Voltaire had completely convinced them of
the utility of his favorite maxim, " strike,
but hide your hand." Their real views were
obvious, indeed, to the more discerning, but
many were duped by what D'Alembert calls,
" *his votes to religion,*" and Voltaire boasts much
of the success of his master stroke of policy,
" in erecting a church, and constantly receiving communion."†

* Barruel's Memoirs, Vol. 1, Chap. 11.   † Ibid.

C H A P. III.

Progress of the Conspiracy ; the Triumph, and Death of the Chiefs.

POWERFUL muft have been the operation of fuch abilities, fubtlety, and zeal. With Frederic of Pruflia, Voltaire clafles, in the number of his adepts, Jofeph II, emperor of Germany, Catharine II, emprefs of Ruflia, Chriftiern VII, king of Denmark, Guftavus III, king of Sweden, Ulrica, queen of Sweden, and Poniatowfki, king of Poland.

Among the princes and princefses, Frederic, landgrave of Heffe Caffel, the Duke of Brunf-wick, Lois Eugene, duke of Wirtemberg, and Lois, prince of Wirtemberg, Charles Theodora, elector palatine, the princefs Anhault Zerbft, and Wilhelmina, margravine of Barieth, are alfo ranked with the initiated.*

* That thefe perfonages were in the habits of a friendly correfpondence with Voltaire, were captivated with his

A great part of the miniſtry, the no-
bleſs, and higher claſs of citizens in France,
and, (excepting the clergy, who for the moſt
part remained firm in the cauſe of religion) the
literati, not of France only, but of Europe
in general, appear to have been enſnared with
this faſcinating philoſophy. Nor was it confined to men of ſcience. Voltaire boaſts,
" That there was not a Chriſtian to be found
from Geneva to Bern ; that Germany gave
him great hopes ; Ruſſia ſtill greater, and that
in Spain as well as Italy a great revolution was
operating in ideas."

It was theſe proſpects of ſucceſs, probably,
which led him to utter that moſt blaſphemous
prediction, " *That in twenty years more, God
will be in a pretty plight.*" *

The amazing influence of theſe writings is
to be found, not in their ſuperior excellence of

abilities, and charmed with the pleaſing ſounds of reaſon
and philoſophy, is undoubted ; but that they wiſhed the
deſtruction of religion, ſeparate from the abuſes of popery, does not appear, unleſs from the boaſtings of the conſpirators. Frederic, Chriſtiern of Denmark, the landgrave of Heſſe, Wilhelmina of Barieth, if no more, are
however to be excepted from this remark. Barruel's
Memoirs, Vol. I. Chap. 12 and 13.

* Barruel's Memoirs, Vol. I. Chap. 18.

any kind, but in the magic founds of reason and philofophy. The hiftorian juftly remarks, that had Voltaire and D'Alembert called themfelves enemies of Chriftianity, they would have been the execration of Europe. But while only calling themfelves philofophers, they are miftaken for fuch. Voltaire, by his fuperior abilities, had gained fuch afcendency in the literary world, that whatever he was pleafed to call philofophy, became current with all whofe abject minds depended on the opinions of others; and Voltaire was very liberal in applying the term to whatever was impious. He boafts of many philofophers in Paris *behind the counter.** What! fhall every

---

* If Voltaire's judgment was not entirely perverted by his enmity to religion, whenever he reflected upon his curious herd of philofophers, he muft have been diverted with the ridiculous idea. A man may, indeed, be ignorant of philofophy, and the liberal arts, and yet be highly refpectable, while his profeffional employment does not render an acquaintance with thefe fubjects neceffary. But for fuch a man to claim the title of philofopher, and to claim it fimply upon the foundation of his ridiculing that holy religion as abfurd, which a Newton, a Locke, an Addifon, a Jones, and fome of the greateft men of every age have believed and defended; if any thing is a proper object of difguft, it is fuch a wretched compound of pride and ignorance. Of fuch philofophers it is emphatically true, " *That profeffing themfelves to be wife, they became fools.*"

wanton coquette ; shall every husband or wife
who scoffs at conjugal fidelity ; shall every son,
who denies the authority of a parent ; the
courtier destitute of morals, and the man who
is a slave to his passions ; shall these be styled
philofophers ?*

As a useful comment on the foregoing ex-
hibition of successful wickedness, we are now
called to witness the closing scene of the
tragic actors.

I beg leave here to remark for myself, that
I feel a sensible concern in republishing this
scene, not to offend against that reverence
which becomes an imperfect creature, in tracing
the awful footsteps of Jehovah ; nor would I
willingly become accessary in promoting an
undue use of providential dispensations. Ever
odious to me is the practice of supporting our
particular opinions and party distinctions, by
a bold and unwarranted application of God's
high and mysterious providence ; and far am
I from wishing to encourage this sentiment,
that men will receive, in this world, according
to their works ; but, that many events in
providence may be, and ought to be confidered, as confirmations of revealed truth, and

* Barruel's Memoirs, Vol. I. Chap. 19.

that God is fometimes *to be known by the judg-ments which he executes,* none, I prefume, who admit the truth of revelation, will deny.

The confpiracy exhibited an inftance un-paralleled in the hiftory of man. In Voltaire we behold, not fimply an unbeliever, a man hurried into finful indulgences by the impulfe of violent appetites, but the bold, active, de-termined enemy of God and religion, deliber-ately devoting his uncommon abilities to the difhonor of the giver, and the feduction of his fellow creatures from their allegiance to their Maker. Did not this mifchief, this com-municated poifon feem to require a powerful antidote? And may we not imagine *compaf-fion* as imploring the Father of his creatures, to afford fome extraordinary means for de-livering the minds of men from the violence they had fuffered, by the perverfion of fuch uncommon talents?

Such is the tendency of the following in-terefting feene. Let the world draw near and receive inftruction! Let mankind duly efti-mate the boafted powers of human reafon, and the fruits of that philofophy, which proudly rejects the offered comforts of the gofpel!

The French government had testified their
disapprobation of Voltaire's writings, by pro-
hibiting his visiting Paris. His numerous
partisans, at length, succeed in procuring a
suspension of this sentence ; and their chief,
now in the eighty fourth year of his age, is
once more permitted to make his appearance
at the capital. The academies and theatres
confer on him their richest honors ; and the
adepts, in his triumph, celebrate their own.
So sensibly did he enjoy this adulation, that he
exclaimed, " *You then wish to make me expire
with glory.*" But whatever was their design,
the will of Providence was very different from
this ; for, in the midst of his triumphs, he was
seized with a violent hemorrhage,* and his
conscience was alarmed with the more insup-
portable terrors of the Almighty. In the first
part of his sickness, he applied to a Romish
priest, and gave in a declaration of his re-
pentance ; but the sophisters interfered, and
prevented its being completed according to
the ritual of that church. Remorse and rage
filled the remainder of his wretched days ;
now supplicating, and now blaspheming that
Saviour whom he had sworn *to crush ;* and in
plaintive accents he would cry out, " Oh

* A violent flux of blood.

Chrift! Oh Jefus Chrift!" And then complain that he was abandoned by God and man. The hand which had traced the fentence of an impious, revelling king, feemed to trace before his eyes, " *Crufh then, do crufh the wretch.*"

" *Begone*," he would exclaim to the confpirators who approached him, " *It is you who have brought me to my prefent ftate, and what a wretched glory have you procured me!*" His phyficians and attendants were compelled, by the horrors of the fcene, to retire. Mr. Tronchin, his principal phyfician, declared, that " *the furies of Aroftes could give but a faint idea of thofe of Voltaire.*"

Thus died, on the 30th of May, 1778, three months after his firft feizure, worn out by his own fury, rather than by difeafe and the decay of years, the moft malignant confpirator againft Chriftianity that had lived fince the time of the apoftles.*

* The above facts are grounded on juridical minutes, depofited at Paris, in the hands of Monf. Momet, Notary Public, and on the teftimony of the celebrated Mr. Tronchin. This teftimony is confirmed by a letter from M. De Luc, fent to Abbe Barruel, after the appearance of the firft volume of thefe Memoirs, and which may be feen in the appendix to the third volume.

F

After the death of Voltaire, D'Alembert
conducted the affairs of the conspiracy, of
which he was proclaimed chief. He died
November 1783, five years after his patron;
and from what can be collected, it appears,
that he derived no better comforts from his
boasted philosophy. Condorcet undertook to
render him inacceffible to all who would willingly declare the truth, and in particular,
violently excluded the Rector of St. Ger-
main's, who prefented himfelf in the quality
of a paftor; yet when firft relating the circumftances of his death, he hefitated not to add,
" *Had I not been there he would have flinched
alfo.*"* The adept, Grim, writing an account
of his death to Frederic, fays, " That ficknefs
had greatly weakened D'Alembert's mind in
his laft moments."

Diderot in his laft ficknefs, upon being
faithfully admonifhed of his danger by a
young man who attended him, melted into
tears; applied to a clergyman, Mr. De Ter-
fac, and was preparing a recantation of his
errors, when his fituation was difcovered by
the fophifters. With much difficulty they
perfuaded him that a country air would

* Hiftorical Dictionary, article D'Alembert.

relieve him. The wretches concealed his departure, and fupported him with thefe delu-
five hopes, when they knew his laft hour was
faft approaching. They watched him till they
had feen him expire, and then reprefented that
he died in all his atheifm, without any figns
of remorfe.

Frederic alone, fucceeded in perfuading
himfelf, that death was an everlafting fleep.[*]

* Barruel's Memoirs, Vol. I. Chap. 18.

CHAP. IV.

OCCULT MASONRY.*

By Occult Masonry is here to be understood those Lodges of Free Masons, which, leaving their original simple institutions, introduced subjects and practices which had no connection with Masonry, and of which the lodges which remained pure, had no knowledge.

* The authorities on which Dr. Robison chiefly relies, to support his narrative (besides the original writings) are,

  1 Grosse Absicht des Illuminaten Ordens.

  2 Nachtrages (3) denselben.

  3 Weishaupt's improved system.

  4 Sytem des Illum. Ordens aus dem Original Schriften gezogen. Rob. p. 162.

  Rev. Dr. J. Erskine, in a letter to a correspondent in New England, dated June 13, 1801, adds his testimony to the authenticity of the books, and most alarming facts to which Dr. Robison refers ; and adds, " I am willing you should make what use of my letter you may think proper."   [Manuscript Letter.]

To exhibit a brief view of what may be collected of importance respecting thefe adulterated Lodges, from Robifon's Proofs and Barruel's Memoirs, is the defign of this chapter. Such a view is a neceffary introduction to the hiftory of Illuminifm, and its connection with the Mafonic orders.

Dr. Robifon obferves, that in the early part of his life he commenced an acquaintance with Mafonry, which he confidered as affording a pretext for fpending an hour or two in decent conviviality. That, though he had been fuccefsful in his mafonic career, and attained fome diftinguifhed degrees, yet he was induced to fufpend his intercourfe with the lodges, viewing Mafonry as an unprofitable amufement, and in a degree inconfiftent with the more ferious duties of life. That while in this ftate of indifference refpecting Free Mafonry, his attention was awakened, and his curiofity excited by fome new circumftances, particularly by what he met with in a German work, called *Religions Begebenheiten,* i. e. *Religious Occurrences,* a periodical work, publifhed by Profeffor Kœefter of Gieffen, which convinced him that Mafonry was applied to purpofes of which he had been wholly ignorant. That he found the lodges the haunts of many projectors in religion and politics, in direct oppofition to that eftablifhed rule in Mafonry, " *That nothing of religion or politics fhall ever be introduced into the lodges,*" and that purfuing the fubject, he found affociations rifing out of thefe abufes, deftructive of religion and fociety. In this work he profeffes the benevolent defign of teaching mankind the danger refulting from thefe combinations ; and left the freedom with which he expofes thefe perverted lodges, fhould be confidered as inconfiftent with his mafonic engagements, he vindicates himfelf by obferving, that he has not divulged the fecrets of original Mafonry, and that he is under no obligations to conceal its abufes, and new invented degrees.*

Abbe Barruel introduces the fubject of Mafonry by bearing a moft honorable teftimony of many lodges, in England in particular, whofe members he confiders as ignorant

* Introduction to Robifon's Proofs. Dr. Robifon, in a letter to a correfpondent in America, dated Sept. 23, 1800, writes, that fince the publication of his book, he has " greatly increafed the body of his evidence, by means of many German publications ;" but that his ill health and official duties, prevent his arranging and publifhing this evidence.

of the real object of the inftitution, which he
pronounces to be radically evil. In fupport
of this idea he attempts to prove, that the
words *liberty and equality*, which are common
to all lodges, imply, not fimply that *Mafonic
Fraternity* of which they are ufually confidered
as expreffive, but what they have been explained to intend in France, during the late
revolution. A *liberty* or fredom from all religious and moral obligation ; an equality fub-
verfive of all focial order and fubordination.

It cannot be expected that his obfervations
on this fubject fhould be introduced here, as
they have no very intimate connection with
the object of our prefent inquiry ; but they
who wifh to become more fully acquainted
with his laborious review and explanation of
mafonic myfteries, may recur to the ninth and
fucceeding chapters in the fecond volume of
his Memoirs. He was himfelf a Mafon ; and
at the fame time not fubject to the cuftomary
bonds of fecrecy. To explain what is fo un-
ufual, he relates, That at the time of his admiffion, Mafonry had become fo frequent in
France, that the fecret was lefs guarded ; that
upon a mafonic occafion, where all the company, except himfelf, were Mafons, and generally his acquaintance and intimate friends,

he was urged to join them, and, in a manner,
forced with them into the lodge ; but, still re-
fusing the proposed oath with great resolution,
his firmness, it was said, proved him a Mason,
and he was accordingly received with great
applauses, and at that time advanced to the
degree of Master.   This gave him peculiar
advantages for treating this subject, and he
appears not to have made a dishonorable use
of the privilege.*

Whatever doubts may be entertained of his
general theory, his investigation affords indubitable proofs of the accommodating nature
of masonic mysteries, and their pliancy to all
the purposes of cabal and intrigue.   Robison's
Proofs forcibly impress the same idea.   In
England the lodge afforded a retreat to the adherents of the Stuarts, and was a covert for
their meetings.   In France it was made sub-
fervient to the views of the British Pretender.
In the lodge of the *Maçon Parfait* is the following device : " A lion wounded by an arrow,
and escaped from the stake to which he had
been bound, with the broken rope still about
his neck, is represented lying at the mouth
of a cave, and occupied with mathematical

* Barruel's Memoirs, Vol. II. p. 152, 155.

inftruments, which are lying near him. A broken crown lies at the foot of the ftake." There can be little doubt but that this emblem alludes to the dethronement, the captivity, the efcape, and afylum of James II, and his hopes of reftoration by the help of the loyal brethren. Great ufe was alfo made of Mafonry by the Church of Rome, for fecuring and extending her influence on the laymen of rank and fortune.*

But this prominent feature of Mafonry, its accommodating nature, will more readily be perceived when we come to notice its eafy coalefcence with the defigns of the Illuminees.

The abufes of Mafonry, which we are now tracing, and which came to their full growth in the Illuminated lodges, appear to have originated in a natural fpirit of inquiry, ftruggling with the reftraints which the French government formerly impofed on a free difcuffion of religion and politics. Under the covert of a lodge, they found themfelves liberated from a painful reftraint, and experienced the pleaf- ure of communicating fentiments in fafety, which, in another place, would have expofed them to danger.

* Robifon's Proofs, p. 28, 31.

We need not be told that even innocent in-
dulgencies are liable to degenerate into the
most pernicious habits. This truth was forcibly exemplified in the French lodges. A
channel being once opened by which the heart
could give vent to its feelings, the small stream
soon became a torrent, affording a passage to
every absurd, sceptical, and disorganizing idea,
and which, in its final progress, not only demolished the superstructures which superstition and despotism had raised, but threatened
to undermine the foundations of religion and
society.

The pliant forms of Masonry were easily
wrought into a compliance with the new
views of the Masons. New explanations were
given, and new degrees invented, which,
while they gave pleasure by the air of mystery
attending them, served as a veil to conceal
from the young adept, a full view of the object towards which he was led. The veil was
gradually removed, as his exercised organs
were strengthened to endure the discovery.

We find a striking instance of the new explanations given to ancient symbols, in the
degrees of *Chevaliers de l'Orient, and Chevaliers
de l'Aigle*, which were once explained as typ-

ical of the life and immortality brought to light by the gofpel ; but a more modern explanation reprefents the whole hiftory and peculiar doctrines of the gofpel, as being typical of the final triumph of reafon and philofophy over error.

To meet the new views of the Mafons, a new feries of degrees was added to the lift, viz. the *Novice*, the *Elû de la Verité*, and the *Sublime Philofophe*. A lively imagination would be gratified by tracing thefe curious allegories ; but the reader muft be fatisfied with one as a fample ; that of the *Chevalier de Soleil*, which was an early addition to the mafonic degrees. I have the rather chofen this inftance, as here Robifon and Barruel appear not to harmonize in their relation. This apparent difagreement, however, vanifhes upon a clofer infpection, which will fhew us that they defcribe different parts of the fame degree.

Robifon confines himfelf to the introductory formula, in which we are to obferve, that the *Tres Venerable* is Adam ; the Senior Warden is Truth ; and all the Brethren are Children of Truth. In the procefs of reception, brother Truth is afked, What is the hour ? He informs father Adam, that among men it

is the hour of darkness, but that it is mid-day
in the lodge. The candidate is asked, Why
he has knocked at the door, and what is become of the eight companions ? He says, that
the world is in darkness, and his companions
and he have lost each other ; that Hesperus,
the star of Europe, is obscured by clouds of
incense, offered up by superstition to despots,
who have made themselves gods, and have
retired into the inmost recesses of their palaces,
that they may not be recognized to be men,
while their priests are deceiving the people,
and causing them to worship these divinities.*

Barruel's account of this degree, contains an
explanation of the implements which the new-
ly received brother finds in the lodge, and the
instructions there given him. A part of these
instructions, which succeed the foregoing introductory explanations, follow.

" By the *Bible* you are to understand, that
you are to acknowledge no other law than
that of Adam, the law that the Almighty en-
graved on his heart, and that is what is called
the *law of nature*. The *compass* recals to your
mind, that God is the central point of every

* Robison's Proofs, p. 33, 35.

thing, from which every thing is equally diftant, and to which every thing is equally near.
By the *fquare* we learn, that God has made
every thing equal ; and by the *Cubic ftone*, that
*all your actions are equal with refpect to the fove-
reign good."*

The moft effential part of this difcourfe is
that which brother Veritas (or Truth) gives
of the degree of the Elect. Among others is
the following paffage : " If you afk me what
are the neceffary qualities to enable a Mafon to
arrive at the center of real perfection, I anfwer,
that to attain it, he maft have crufhed the
head of the ferpent of worldly ignorance, and
have caft off thofe prejudices of youth concerning the myfteries of the predominant religion
of his native country. *All religious worfhip being only invented in hopes of acquiring power, and to
gain precedency among men ; and by a floth which
covets, under the falfe pretence of piety, its neighbor's
riches.* This, my dear brother, is what you
have to combat ; fuch is the monfter you have
to crufh under the emblem of the ferpent. *It
is a faithful reprefentation of that which the ignorant vulgar adore, under the name of religion."**
Such doctrines need no comment.

G

* Barruel's Memoirs. Vol. II. p. 163.

With thefe new degrees and explanations,
the French lodges appear to have undergone
fome new modifications with refpect to their
connection and correfpondence with each other.   The *Bienfaifants*, at Lyons, rofe into high
reputation.   This lodge feems to have taken
the lead in the diforganizing fentiments of the
day, and was acknowledged as a parent lodge
by feveral foreign focieties.   But the moft diftinguifhed, was the *Grand Orient*, at Paris. This
may be confidered, rather as a *Mafonic Parlia-
ment*, compofed of delegates from all the principal lodges, and in which mafonic concerns
were ultimately determined.   In 1782 this fociety had under its direction 266 improved
lodges ; the whole united under the Duke of
Orleans as Grand Mafter, at leaft apparently,
but really guided by the moft profound adepts,
who made ufe of his intereft and influence to
promote their views, and then refigned him to
that deftruction, which was pronounced juft,
by the unanimous vote of mankind.*

While the lodges in France were pafling
this metamorphofis, thofe in Germany retained their original, fimple conflitutions, which

* Barruel's Memoirs, Vol. II. p. 239 ; and Robifon's
Proofs, p. 37, 48.

they firſt received from England, in 1716. It is remarkable that the Germans had been long accuſtomed to the *word*, the *ſign*, and the *gripe* of the Maſons; and there are extant, and in force, borough laws, enjoining the maſters of Maſons to give employment to journeymen who had the proper word and ſign. But the firſt German lodge, was eſtabliſhed at Cologne, in the year abovementioned.

The Germans, always fond of the marvellous, had attributed ſtrange powers to Maſonry, and been ſeeking, with their characteriſtic patience, the power of tranſmuting metals, of raiſing ghoſts, and other wonderful ſecrets which they imagined were concealed in maſonic myſteries. This diſpoſition had rendered them the dupes of Hunde, Johnſon, Stark, and other adventurers who found their advantages in German credulity.

But about the year 1757, an entire revolution took place. Some French officers, then reſiding at Berlin, undertook to communicate to the Germans their refinements in Maſonry. They could not reſiſt the enchantment of the ribbands and ſtars with which the French had decorated the order. A Mr. Roſa, a French commiſſary, brought from Paris a complete

waggon load of mafonic ornaments, which
were all diftributed before it had reached Berlin, and he was obliged to order another to
furnifh the lodges of that city. The mafonic
fpirit was revived throughout Germany : All
were eager to hear and learn. New degrees
were invented, and Mafonry underwent a general revolution. All proclaiming the excel-
lencies of Mafonry ; while not one could tell
in what its excellency confifted ; their zeal
but ferved to increafe their confufion and diforder.

Thofe who believed that mafonic myfteries
concealed the wonderful powers of magic and
alchymy, engaged, with frefh zeal, in chafe of
the airy phantom ; and frefh adventurers appeared, who, in their turn, raifed and difappointed the hopes of their admirers. Happy
would it have been, had no worfe confequences enfued than the wafte of their time and
money in the purfuit of thefe fooleries ; but
thefe French inftructors, together with their
new forms and degrees, had communicated
new notions refpecting government and religion, and introduced the cuftom of harangu-
ing on thefe fubjects in the lodges. A clofe
connection was formed between the French
and fome of the German lodges, and the for-

mer were not unwilling to communicate their new difcoveries. Philofophically illuminated, the German adepts began to difcern, that religion was the flavery of the free born mind ; that reafon was the only fafe guide, and the only deity whom mankind ought to worfhip ; that the eftablifhment of government was the original fin ; and emancipation from all legal reftraint, the true regeneration taught by Jefus Chrift ; and which can be effected only by the wonderful power of thofe two words, *liberty* and *equality.**

The reader, who has not been acquainted with the hiftory of modern philofophy, will hardly believe, perhaps, that this is a ferious ftatement of facts, or find it eafy to conceive that fuch abfurdities were ever dignified with the title of philofophy. But thefe fentiments are all to be found in the code of the Illuminees ; and to poffefs the mind with thefe fentiments, is the grand defign of that fyftem of policy expreffed by Illuminifm ; the hiftory of which will be given in the fucceeding chapters.

G 2

* Robifon's Proofs, p. 63, 75.

It is proper to obferve here, that at this time, Baron Knigge, refided in the neighborhood of Franckfort, who from his youth had been an enthufiaft in Mafonry, and a believer in its cabaliftic powers. Defpairing, at length, of ever finding the Philofopher's Stone, in purfuit of which his father had fpent his fortune, and he his time, his enthufiafm was now diverted into another channel. The feeptical difcourfes delivered in the lodges, affifted him to difcover that Mafonry was pure natural religion, and that the whole duty of man was comprifed in Cofmopolitifm, or facrificing all private interefts for the promotion of univerfal happinefs. Inflamed with thefe romantic ideas, he labored to propagate them through the lodges.

The authority affumed by the lodges of Berlin, had difgufted many of their brethren, and produced divifions, which were further increafed by a variety of adventurers, each of which had his adherents. The Baron, found thefe circumftances a bar to his fuccefs, for the removal of which he projected a general congrefs from all the mafonic focieties in Europe and America. The deranged fituation of mafonic concerns feemed to render fuch a meeting expedient; and by the affiftance of the lodges of Franckfort and Wetzlar it was obtained, and held at Willemsbad, in 1780. Here deputies, affembled from the four quar-ters of the globe, were bufied for fix months, debating about the myfteries of Mafonry with all the ferioufnefs of ftate ambaffadors.

While Knigge was laboring to poffefs the deputies with his fentiments, he was met by another Mafon, the Marquis of Conftanza, who convinced him that his new ideas refpect-ing Mafonry had been reduced to a regular fyftem, and were now rapidly fpreading in feveral mafonic focieties. Tranfported with this difcovery, he eagerly united himfelf to the Illuminees, which was the fect to which the Marquis introduced him, and joined his efforts with thofe of his new inftructor to gain over deputies, and to give a direction to the proceedings of the convention favorable to the defigns of the Illuminees.

In thefe attempts they were not without fuccefs. Numbers entered fully into their views, and the general refult of the congrefs was agreeable to their wifhes. It was decreed, that any Mafon of the three firft degrees fhould be admitted to every lodge of whatever defcription ; which opened all the lodges to the agents of Illuminifm. It was alſo decreed, that every lodge ſhould have the liberty of de-claring to which grand lodge it would be fub-ject. The plan of union was termed Eclectic, which was alſo favorable to the new order, as it was in lodges of that denomination that it began its exiſtence.*

We ſhall now proceed to take a view of that memorable ſociety, in which all the Anti-Chriſtian, and Anti-Social opinions of the day were reduced to a regular fyſtem, and propa-gated with a zeal worthy of a better caufe.

* I lately met with the following remark, in a letter from Profeſſor Ebeling, which I beg leave to introduce for the ſatisfaction of thoſe who may be diſpoſed to doubt the above repreſentation of Germanic Maſonry. "Ma-ſonry (he writes) was much in vogue in Germany from the year 1740 to 1760, but made no noiſe ; but in later years the Maſonry of Germany was ſtrangely corrupted ; diviſions aroſe, of which Robiſon ſpeaks pretty exact as far as I know."

* Robiſon's Proofs, p. 76, 83   Barruel's Memoirs, Vol. IV. p. 101, 104.

C H A P. V.

ILLUMINISM. Its Origin, Actors, and different Grades.

THE lodge Theodore, of Munich in Bavaria, was the moft remarkable of the Eclectic lodges ; and had formed a conftitution of its own, in confequence of inftructions received from the lodge Bienfaifants at Lyons. Diftinguifhed among the members of this lodge, was Dr. Adam Weifhaupt, Profeffor of Canon Law in the Univerfity at Ingolftadt. He had acquired a high reputation in his profefiion, which drew around him numbers from the neighboring Univerfities. The advantages which thefe circumftances gave him for impreffing his own views upon the minds of youth, perhaps firft fuggefted to him the idea of becoming the leader of a more numerous fociety, and it certainly was the means of his fuccefs in fpreading his pernicious fentiments.

The bold opinions in religion and politics,
which were more openly taught in the lodge
Theodore than in any other, and which Knigge
labored to propagate, Weishaupt was the first
to reduce to a regular code. His scheme appears to be calculated, not so much for uniting
persons of similar sentiments in one society,
as for seducing those of opposite inclinations,
and by a most artful and detestable process,
gradually obliterating from their minds every
moral and religious sentiment. It is in this
view principally that this plan of seduction calls
for the attention of mankind, as it developes
the secret, insidious policy by which the agents
of faction and infidelity lead on their disciples,
still concealing their real designs, until the
mind is involved in a maze of error, or
entangled in snares from which there is no
retreat.

Another trait which deserves particular notice in this prime theory of deception, is that
artful structure by which the deluded victim is
led to give his support to a system, which, in
its invisible operation, is undermining the object of his fondest attachment. Persons have
subscribed to this constitution who, had they
been aware of its tendency and issue, would

fooner have committed their hand to the flame.*

What thofe particulars were in Weifhaupt's early life, which were confeffedly " great de-viations from pure morality," we are not told; but the hiftory of his illuminated career, and his conduct while he fuftained the dignified of-fice of a profeffor in a Univerfity, certainly give us no favorable idea of that part of his life, which is acknowledged to be immoral.

We here lay before the reader a letter, found among the original writings of the Illu-minees in Bavaria, from Weifhaupt to Hertel Canon of Munich, but under the feigned names of *Spartacus* to *Marius*.

" SEPTEMBER, 1783.

" Now let me, under the moft profound fe-crecy, lay open the fituation of my heart ; I am almoft defparate. My honor is in danger, and I am on the eve of lofing *that reputation which gave me fo great an authority over our people. My fifter in law is with child.* How fhall I reftore the honor of a perfon who is the victim of a

---

* Robifon's Proofs, p. 82, 85. Barruel's Memoirs, Vol. III. Chap. 1.

crime that is wholly mine ? *We have already
made several attempts to destroy the child ;* she was
determined to undergo all ; but Euriphon is too
timid.   Could I depend on Celfe's fecrecy,
(Profeſſor Buder at Munich) he could be of
great fervice to me ; *he had promiſed me his aid
three years ago.* Mention it to him if you think
proper.   If you could extricate me from this
unfortunate ſtep, you would reſtore me to life,
to reſt, to honor, and to authority. If you
cannot, I forewarn you of it, *I will hazard a
defperate blow*, for I neither can nor will loſe
my honor. I know not what devil * * * [Here
decency obliges us to be ſilent.] It is not too
late to make an attempt, for ſhe is only in her
fourth month. Do think of fome means which
can extricate me from this affair.

I am yours,
Spartacus."

Other letters to different perfons upon the
fame ſubject, and of a fimilar import, were
found with this. Though he had folemnly
denied his having uſed, or even being acquainted with means of abortion ; yet, when the
matter became puolic, he admits the facts refpecting his fifter in law, and the attempt to
deſtroy the child, but juſtifies himſelf with an
effrontery which diſcovers ſtill more than the

crime itself, a mind loft to every fentiment of
goodnefs. " This," he fays, " is far from proving any depravity of heart. In his condition,
his honor at ftake, what-elfe was left him to
do ? His greateft enemies, the Jefuits, have
taught, that in fuch a cafe it is lawful to make
way with the child. In the introductory fault,
he has the example of the beft of men. The
fecond was its natural confequence ; it was altogether involuntary ; and, in the eye of a
philofophical judge, who does not fquare himfelf by the harfh letters of a blood thirfty law-
giver, he has but a very trifling account to
fettle."*

In connection with the character of the
founder of the fect, it may be proper to bring
into view, thofe of his Areopagites, in whom
he principally confided, and who were feated
next himfelf in the government of the fociety.
He himfelf furnifhes the portrait in a letter to
Cato, (Zwack.)

"I have received," he writes, " the moft fatal
intelligence from Thebes. They have given

H

a public scandal, by admitting into the lodges
that vile *Propertius*, a libertine, loaded with
debts, and a most detestable being. Our *So-
crates*, who could be of the greatest use to us,
is always drunk ; our *Augustus* has acquired
the worst of reputations ; the brother *Alcibiades* is perpetually sighing and pining away at
the feet of his landlady ; *Tiberius* attempted
to lay violent hands on Diomede's sister, and
suffered himself to be caught by the husband ;
Heavens ! what men have I got for Areopagites !"

It appears that it was not the detestable nature of these actions which excited his disgust,
but their influence on the reputation of his
order, for he further writes, " Judge your-
selves what would be the consequence, if such
a man as our Marcus Aurelius (Feder) were
once to know what a *set of men, destitute of morals ; what a set of debauchees, liars, spendthrifts,
bragadocios, and fools, replete with vanity and pride,
you have among you, &c."* *

From several expressions in his letters, it
appears that Weishaupt had, for a considerable
time, been meditating the plan of an order
which should in time govern the world ; but

* Robison's Proofs, p. 114.

it was not fully completed when he first put his fyftem in operation, and inftituted the *order of the Illuminees.* This was done in May, 1776, by the initiation of two of his Univerfity pupils; but the order was not fully eftablifhed till 1778.[*]

Weifhaupt's aim in the frequent reviews, and nice touches which he gave his plan, was firft, to explore every avenue to the heart, every procefs by which he might moft effectually feduce, and lead men blindfold; and in the next place, to provide fufficiently for his own fecurity; for, notwithftanding the fentence of banifhment which he was under drew from him the moft grievous complaints of defpotic cruelty, he confidered it a much lighter punifhment than that which awaited him in cafe of detection.

In a letter to Cato, he writes, " I daily put to the teft what I made laft year, and I find that my performances of this year are far fuperior. You know the fituation in which I ftand. It is abfolutely neceffary that I fhould, during my life, remain unknown to the

* Robifon's Proofs, p. 107. Barruel's Memoirs, Vol. III. Chap. 1, Ibid. Vol. IV. p. 55, 56.

greater part of the adepts themselves. *I am often overwhelmed with the idea that all my meditations, all my services and toils are, perhaps, only twisting a rope, or planting a gallows for myself.* *

The following scheme exhibits the different grades through which the candidate progresses to the perfection of Illumination.

NURSERY.	{		Preparation, Novice, Minerval, Illumin. Minor.	
MASONRY.	{	*Symbolic.*	{	Apprentice, Fellowcraft, Master.
		Scotch.	{	Illum. Major, Novice, Illum. Dirigens, Knight.
MYSTERIES.	{	*Lesser.*	{	Presbyter, Priest, Prince, Regent.
		Greater.	{	Magus, Rex.†

There is a part common to all these degrees, viz. that of the Insinuator, or Recruitor; the duty of whose office is to find and bring forward members for the first and succeeding degrees.‡

* Barruel's Memoirs, Vol. III. p. 12.   † Ibid. p. 19.
‡ Robison's Proofs, p. 139.

C H A P. VI.

The Code of the Illuminees.

IT was neceffary that fome members of the order fhould be known as fuch, that they might ferve as guides to thofe who fhould have a defire to be initiated. Thefe are the *Minervals*, who are the only vifible members of the fociety. A candidate for admiffion muft make his wifh known to fome Minerval; he reports it to a fuperior, by whom, in an appointed channel, it is communicated to the council. No farther notice is taken of it for fome time. The candidate is obferved in filence, if judged unfit for the order no notice is taken of his requeft ; but if otherwife, he receives privately an invitation to a conference, and upon figning the declaration required of the preparation clafs, is admitted to the Noviciate.*

H 2

* Robifon's Proofs, p. 94.

But the *Insinuators* are the principal agents for propagating the order. These are invisible *spies, seeking whom they may devour*, who enter on their tablets, with which they are always to be furnished, the names of such as they judge would be useful to the order, with the reasons for or against their admission.

The instructions of the insinuator teach him to look after young men from eighteen to thirty, those in particular who have not completed their education, and those whose exterior prepossesses one in their favor. His attention is likewise directed to men of rank, wealth, and influence. Men of an insinuating, intriguing disposition, mechanics of all professions, booksellers, school masters, post masters, those who keep post horses, and the discontented of every class of people.

Of these minutes the Insinuator is required to make a return twice every month to his superiors, who form a list of such as they judge suitable prey, and put it into the hands of an Insinuator, not the one perhaps who sent in the name, but one whom the superiors of the order shall see fit to appoint. And he now begins the labor of gaining over his pupil to the society. The person thus marked

as the object of seduction, though he has ex-
pressed no desire of uniting with the order, is
placed in the grade of

Preparation. It would be a task indeed to
trace minutely the arts of insinuation, and the
cautious steps by which the Recruiter is to
proceed. In general, the curiosity of the subject is to be excited by suggestions, made as
by accident, of the existence and power of
such a society ; his mind is to be impressed
with the most honorable views of the design of
this institution ; his affections and confidence
are to be gained by every art of insinuation ;
the power of secret societies, and the pleasure
of secretly reigning, are to be presented to his
imagination, and books provided by the society, and corresponding with its views, are to be
put into his hands. Should he break from all
these snares, he is marked for an enemy whose
character and influence the society is henceforth concerned to destroy. *They must be
gained, or ruined in the public opinion, is the law of
the order.* But should the candidate, by these
arts, be led to express a desire to join this invisible combination, he is required to subscribe
an express and solemn declaration, " never to
reveal, by sign, word, or any other way, even
to the most intimate friend, whatever shall be

entrufted to him relative to his entrance into
a fecret fociety, and this whether his reception
take place or not ; and that he fubjects himfelf
to this fecrecy the more willingly, *as his intro-
ducer affures him, that nothing is ever tranfacted in
this fociety hurtful to religion, morals or the ftate.*"*
The candidate having fubfcribed this declaration commences

Novice. He is now introduced to an inftructor, the only one perhaps of the order
whom he is permitted to know. By this inftructor he is taught, *that filence and fecrecy are
the very foul of the order,* and enjoined never to
fpeak of any thing belonging to it, even before thofe whom he may fuppofe to be initiated, without the ftrongeft neceffity. He is
alfo furnifhed with a new fupply of books and
writings, calculated for his advancement.

Here a cautionary direction is introduced,
which extends to all the different degrees, that
if any of the brotherhood fall fick, the other
brethren are to vifit him, to prevent his making any unfavorable declarations, and to fecure any papers with which he may have been
entrufted.

* Robifon's Proofs, p. 94. Barruel's Memoirs, Vol. III.
Chap. 3.

To qualify the Novice for the practice of that fecrecy which has been reprefented as of fuch importance, he is furnifhed with what may be called the *Dictionary of Illuminifm*. He here learns that no brother bears the fame name in the order which he does in the world. He receives a name for himfelf, and is made acquainted with that of his inftructor, and with thofe of the other brethren, as he is admitted to know them.

The following is a brief fample of this vocabulary. The fictitious name of Weifhaupt, was *Spartacus* ; of Knigge, *Philo ;* of the Marquis Conftanza, *Diomedes ;* of Zwack, *Cato ;* of Baron Baffus, *Hannibal ;* of Count Savioli, *Brutus ;* of Nicolai, *Lucian ;* of Count Maffenhaufen, *Ajax ;* of Councellor Hoheneicher, *Alcibiades ;* of Merz, *Tiberius ;* &c.*

The Novice is alfo put upon the ftudy of a new *Geography*, from which he learns, that places, as well as perfons, bear a new name. Bavaria, is denominated *Achaia*, and Auftria *Egypt ;* Munich is called *Athens*, and Vienna, *Rome*, &c.

* Barruel's Memoirs, Vol. III. Chap. 4. and Vol. IV. p. 173. Robifon's Proofs, p. 160.

Time too, he finds, has undergone a new arrangement, and he must again study his calendar. The Persian era, beginning A. D. 630, is adopted by the Illuminees. The months are known by new names, and are of very different lengths ; Pharavardin has no less than forty one days, while Afphandar has only twenty.

Nor is the candidate yet qualified to correspond with his new brethren, until he has acquired the cypher of the order. A simple one is prepared for the lower grades, but the superiors make use of hieroglyphics.

He now begins the study of the statutes of the society, and a morality extracted from heathen writers ; but is told that the knowledge of mankind is above all other things important, and to acquire this, tracing characters, and noticing occurrences, are strenuously recommended ; his observations are to be submitted to the review of his superiors.

In this stage of his noviciate, he is required to present the order with a written account of his name, place of birth and residence, age, rank, profession, favorite studies, books, secret writings, revenues, friends, enemies, parents, &c. A fimilar table is prepared by his inftructor, of whatever he has been able to difcover ; and from a comparifon of thefe, and his anfwers to a number of interefting queftions, the fuperiors judge of the expedi‑ ency of admitting him to the laft proofs.

His admiffion being agreed upon, in the dead of the night he is led to a gloomy apart‑ ment, and being repeatedly queftioned re‑ fpecting his readinefs to devote himfelf to the order, he confirms his confent with a folemn oath, of which the following is a part, " *I vow an eternal filence, an inviolable obedience and fidelity to all my fuperiors, and to the ftatutes of the order. With refpect to what may be the object of the order, I fully and abfolutely renounce my own penetration, and my own judgment.* I promife to look upon the interefts of the order as my own ; and as long as I fhall be a member of it, *I promife to ferve it with my life, my honor, and my eftates.*" Having figned this oath, and with a fword pointed at his breaft, being threatened with unavoidable vengeance, from which no potentate on earth can defend him, fhould he betray the order, he commences

Minerval, and becomes a member of a

lodge.* Here illuminism commences its connection with Masonry ; and here those, who
do not discover a disposition fully compliant
with the views of their guides, are left to
divert themselves with the three degrees of
apprentice, fellowcraft, and master, and never
attain any further acquaintance with Illuminism. But this, it was found, would not sat-
isfy all candidates, and in particular, those
who had previously been members of lodges ;
       intermediate degrees were therefore add-
       the minor and major Illuminee, and
       Knight.

The Minervals hold frequent meetings under the direction of some more illuminated
superior. These meetings are professedly devoted to literary pursuits, but particular care
is taken to give the discussions a direction
which shall coincide with the designs of Illuminism. *That suicide is lawful under pressing
dangers and calamities ; that the end sanctifies the
means,* or that theft and murder become com-
mendable when committed to advance a good
cause, are sentiments frequently brought into
view in the meetings of the Minervals. From
these discussions the superiors judge of the

* Barruel's Memoirs, Vol. III Chap 4.

propriety of advancing the candidate to the next degree, which is that of[*]

Illuminatus Minor. The members of this clafs have meetings fimilar to thofe of the former degree, but their inftructors are taken only from among thofe who have attained the rank of prieft, and who are directed to labor to remove what, in the language of Illuminifm, is termed political and religious prejudices. The candidates are now to be formed for ufeful laborers. They are put upon ftudying the fecret arts of controling the mind, of feizing the favorable moment, of difcovering and addreffing the ruling paffion, of acquiring a pliancy and verfatility of addrefs, and of concealing their views and feelings from others. As they are found qualified, they have more or lefs of the minerval degree committed to their infpection.

Previous to his advancement to the next degree, the candidate is fubjected to another fcrutinizing examination refpecting his views, and devotednefs to the interefts of Illuminifm.

I

[*] Robifon's Proofs, p. 98. Barruel's Memoirs, Vol. III. Chap. 5.

He is likewise required to give the order a
new proof of his confidence, by exhibiting
an exact record of his whole life written without reservation. The design of the Institutor
in requiring this, appears from his own remarks on this part of his code; " *Now I hold
him ; if he should wish to betray us, we have also
his secrets.*"

The history which the candidate gives of
himself, is compared with the one already
formed, in the records of the order, from
the returns made by his Instructor, and the
discoveries of invisible spies, in which, every
thing relating to his character, abilities, weaknesses, passions, prospects, attachments, aver-
sions, education, and even language, gait,
and physiognomy, are noticed in perhaps fif-
teen hundred particulars. To impress the
mind of the adept with the strongest sense of
the activity of the order, and the folly of
expecting to escape its vigilance, this portrait
of himself is put into his hands, and he is
again questioned respecting his disposition to
unite with such a society.

The disposition of the candidate being
founded by a new series of questions, and having repeated the former oaths of secrecy, and

devotednefs to the order, he paffes through the initiating forms, by which he becomes*

Illuminatus Major, or Scotch Novice. It is impoffible, I find, in this brief fketch, to give a full view of the flow, artful, and infidious procefs by which the mind is powerfully, though infenfibly, drawn from the poffeffion of its former principles, and fired with a fanciful idea of foon attaining the regions of fublime wifdom.

The adept has ftill an Inftructor, who now calls him to attend to the miferies under which mankind are groaning, and the inefficacy of all the means ufed for their relief. This is attributed to the reftraints to which they are fubjected by princes and the priefthood. The importance of *furrounding the powers of the earth with invifible agents, and infenfibly binding their hands,* and the neceffity of union among the friends of fuffering humanity, to accomplifh this defirable end, are ftrongly inculcated. The tractable pupil has but one grade more to afcend before he enters the fecrets of Illuminifm. This is termed by the fect the†

* Robifon's Proofs, p. 102—106. Barruel's Memoirs, Vol. III. Chap. 6 and 7.

† Barruel's Memoirs, Vol. III. Chap. 7.

Scotch Knight. In the late mafonic revolution, this new degree, which had been brought from France, was adopted by feveral of the German lodges. The welcome reception which thofe of this degree met with in all the lodges, determined the Illuminees to unite it with their fystem. This becomes a *Sta bene*, or ftationary degree, to fuch as they fee fit to advance above the ordinary degrees of Mafonry, but are not judged worthy of being admitted to the higher fecrets.

Inftead of the fcenes of darknefs and horror which attended the introduction to the other degrees, the candidate is now introduced into a fplendid lodge, where all the Knights are prefent in the habiliments of their order ; and here, he is told, is a part of thofe unknown legions, united by indiffoluble bands, to defend the caufe of humanity.

In the courfe of the ceremonies, *Jefus Chrift is declared to be the grand mafter of the order*, the enemy of fuperftition, and afferter of reafon ; and in commemoration of him, a mock reprefentation is exhibited of the Lord's Supper.

The inftructions given the new Knight, direct him to promote the increafe of Eclectic

Mafonry ; to endeavor to gain an afcendancy in all other mafonic lodges, either to reform or deftroy them; and, as far as pofible, to convert their funds to the advancement of the caufe of Illuminifm.*

Here we come to the door which leads to the myfteries of Illuminifm ; and here we muft leave behind all thofe, who, though pleafed with romantic ideas of Cofmopolitifm, and of undermining what appeared to them fuperftition, and who, under thefe impreffions, might actively difcharge the inftructions laft received, yet were not to be trufted with the higher myfteries of Illuminifm.

The reader will naturally conclude, that all who were admitted to this order, were not fubjected to thefe tedious preparatory forms ; fome were found (as Knigge for inftance) who met the warmeft wifhes of the fociety, and without any preparation were introduced to its myfteries.

I 2

* Proofs, p. 141 to 145. Memoirs, Vol. III. Chap. 9.

C H A P. VII.

The Mysteries and Government of the Order.

WE must not expect, on entering these
secret chambers, to find the veil which con-
ceals the real designs of the Illuminees wholly
removed. The terrifying impressions of the
rope, which Weishaupt was so conscious of
meriting, kept him much behind the curtain.
This induced him to divide his mysteries into
the *lesser* and the *greater*, each of which have two
departments, one relating chiefly to Religion,
and the other to Politics. The first degree in
the lesser mysteries is that of the

Epopt, or *Priest*. As introductory to this
degree, several questions are proposed to the
candidate, which imply, that no religion,
government, or civil association on earth,
corresponds with the wants of mankind;
and that secret societies are the safe, and only effectual remedies to supply this defect.
He is asked, and the question merits the

confideration of thofe who ridicule the appre-
henfion of danger from Illuminifm, " *Have
you any idea of fecret focieties ; of the rank they held,
or the parts they perform in the events of this
world? Do you view them as infignificant and tran-
fient meteors?* O brother ! God and Nature
had their admirable ends in view, and they
make ufe of thefe fecret focieties as the only,
and as the indifpenfible, means of conducting
us thither. *Thefe fecret fchools of philofophy fhall
one day retrieve the fall of human nature, and
princes and nations fhall difappear from the face of
the earth, and that without any violence. Reafon
fhall be the only book of laws, the fole code of man."*

The object of the fecret of Jefus, he is told,
was to reinftate mankind in their original liberty and equality, but that this fecret was difclofed only to a few. In proof of this he
quotes thefe words of Chrift. " To you is
given to know the myftery of the kingdom
of God ; but to them that are without, all
things are done in parables."*

This doctrine, the profelyte is then told, is
the origin of Mafonry, and the true explanation of its hieroglyphics. The rough ftone of

* Mark, iv. 11.

Mafonry, is the fymbol of the primitive ftate
of man, favage, but free. The ftone fplit,
reprefents the ftate of fallen nature, of mankind divided according to their ftates, governments, or religions.

On this occafion the profelyte, previous to
his receiving the prieftly unction, is invefted
with a white tunic ; the fleeve is tied at the
extremity and middle with bandages of fcarlet,
and he wears a broad filken belt of the fame
color. This drefs is particularly defcribed, becaufe it was in a fimilar one that, during the
French revolution, a comedian appeared perfonally attacking Almighty God, faying, "No !
thou doft not exift. If thou haft power over
the thunder bolts, grafp them ; aim them at
the man who dares fet thee at defiance in the
face of thy altars. But no, I blafpheme thee,
and I ftill live. No, thou doft not exift."*
The next degree in the leffer myfteries is that
of the

Regent. As preparatory to the introduction of the candidate to this degree, he
is brought to the lodge in the habit of a flave
loaded with chains. " It is inquired, who
reduced him to that moft miferable of all con-

* Proofs, p. 145 to 151. Memoirs, Vol. III. Chap. 10.

ditions? It is anfwered, fociety, governments, the fciences, and falfe religion. A voice from within denies him entrance, declaring, that none but freemen can enter there. His guide then anfwers for him, that his will is to be free; that he has been illuminated; flies from his tyrants, and feeks refuge among freemen."

It is needlefs to detail the hacknied fentiments found in the inftructions given on this occafion, as, excepting the mode of expreffing them, they are very fimilar to thofe which have been already mentioned, and which will be found in their private correfpondence lefs veiled in myftery.

One part of thefe inftructions, however, arrefts the attention, which follows; " The great ftrength of our order lies in its concealment; let it never appear in any place in its own name, but always covered by another name, and another occupation. *None is fitter than the three lower degrees of Free Mafonry; the public is accuftomed to it, expects little from it, and therefore takes little notice of it. Next to this, the form of a literary fociety is beft fuited to our purpofes."*

Upon the admiffion of the Regent, his former oaths and fecrets are relinquifhed, with

an expression of entire confidence in his firmnefs ; and in return he gives the order an inftrument, legally executed, by which they are
empowered, in cafe of his deceafe, to claim
any private papers with which he may be
entrufted.*

Such were the lefter myfteries of the Illuminees. Thofe which they term the greater,
were likewife diftinguifhed into thofe of *Majus*, or Philofopher, and *Rex*, or Man King.
Thefe degrees were not found with the other
writings ; and the caufe appears in a letter
from Spartacus (Weifhaupt) to Cato, in
which, fpeaking of one of his higher degrees,
he fays, "I never fuffer it to go out of my hands.
It is of too ferious an import." Philo, (Knigge)
who it feems affifted in forming the higher
degrees, writes to the fame perfon ; " I have
made ufe of fuch precaution in the degrees of
of Epopt, and of Regent, that I fhould not be
afraid of conferring them on Kings or Popes,
provided they had undergone the proper previous trials. In our laft myfteries we have
acknowledged this *pious fraud.*"†

---

* Proofs, p. 151 to 154. Memoirs, Vol. III. Ch. 11, 15.

† Barruel's Memoirs, Vol. III. Chap. 12.

Dr. Robison here quotes the publisher of the Neuefte Arbitung, and Grollman ; and Abbe Barruel quotes Biederman, and a writer, who had left his name with the editors of the Eudemonia, (a Journal printed at Franckfort on the Main) to be published if neceffary, who all profefs to have read thefe degrees, and unite in their teftimony, " that in the degree of *Majus* the doctrines are the fame with thofe of Spinoza, where all is material. God and the world are the fame thing, and all religions are reprefented as chimerical, and the invention of ambitious men." The fecond degree, or *Rex*, teaches, " that every citizen, or houfeholder is a fovereign, as in the Patriarchal ftate ; that all authority, and all magiftracy muft be deftroyed, and that democratic governments are not more confonant with nature than any others."*

The reader doubtlefs will remark the inconfiftency between thefe fentiments upon government, and the attempt which Weifhaupt was then making to render the government of the Illuminees univerfal and abfolute. All that appears to remove this inconfiftency, is to be found under the degree of Regent,

* Proofs, p. 158. Mem. Vol. III. Ch. 12. and Note.

where, in a ſeries of queſtions, the candidate
is led to ſay, " That mankind ought to think
themſelves happy in having *ſuperiors of tried
merit;* and who, unknown to each other, could
not poſſibly ſupport each other in treaſonable
combinations againſt the general welfare ; and
that, ſuppoſing *deſpotiſm* were to enſue, it *could
not be dangerous* in the hands of men, who from
the very firſt ſtep we took in the order,
taught us nothing but *ſcience, liberty and
virtue."* *

Having thus traced the artful proceſs by
which Weiſhaupt led his diſciples to expect,
like the deluded parents of our race, *to become
as Gods,* but which, in fact, was calculated to
deprive them of light, truth, and rightcouſ-
neſs ; we here ſubjoin a brief view of the
arrangement and governmental regulations
of the ſociety. At the head of the order,
however extenſive, is the

General ; to whom regular returns are to
be made of whatever relates to its general,
or more particular intereſts. A conſtant communication and correſpondence is to be pre-
ſerved between him and the

* Barruel's Memoirs, Vol. III. p. 133.

Arcopagites, or council of twelve, who com-
pofe the next degree in the general government. The General of the order is to be
elected by this council, and from their own
number, and to them only is he known, except to fuch immediate confidents, agents, and
fecretaries as he fhall fee fit to employ. The
bufinefs of this fupreme council is to receive
the returns that are made, and prepare them
for the infpection of the General ; and they
are particularly directed to " project and examine plans to be adopted for gradually ena-
bling the fociety to attack the enemy of reafon and human nature, *perfonally.*" Next in
office is the

National Director ; who fuftains the fame
relation to the Illuminees of a particular nation, which the General does to the whole order. The views of the fociety were not confined to one nation. He too, as the General,
has his council of twelve.* Subordinate to
him are the

Provincials, who have the direction of the
affairs of the order in the feveral provinces.

'K

* Barruel's Memoirs, Vol. III. Chap. 18.

The Provincial is empowered to assemble such regents of his province as he shall choose to assist in council.* The next in dignity, though not in the direct line of the general arrangement, is the

Dean. He is chosen by the Epopts, and presides in their academy. The

Epopts, or *Priests,* form a curious and important part in the general system. From this class is formed an academy or chamber of science, consisting of their most learned men in the various arts and sciences. The persons composing this academy, were to be supported by the funds of the society, that they might devote their time to the objects of their appointment. All questions of difficulty proposed by any of the inferior degrees, were required to be given in writing, to their immediate superiors, and by them transmitted to the academy for solution; from thence, in the same channel, the querist received his answer, but from a source to him unknown. The reader will observe the tendency of this institution to promote the literary reputation of the order, and to persuade the adept that

* Perrault's Memoirs, Vol. III, Chap. 17.

he is connected with the fountain head of science.

" *The Occult Sciences*," form one branch particularly recommended to the attention of the academy, under which is comprehended. " The study of the oriental tongues, and others little known; secret methods of writing, and the art of decyphering; *the art of raising the seals of the letters of others*, and of preserving their own from similar practices; the study of ancient and modern hieroglyphics, of secret societies, masonic systems, &c.* Subordinate to the Provincial, in a direct line, we find the

Prefects, each of which may have the inspection of eight lodges, in whose meetings they are required to preside. To these, principally, is entrusted the care of the lower part of the edifice.

The regents alone are eligible to the above offices; and those of this degree who have no particular appointments, are charged with the general inspection of the lower orders, and to study the advancement of the interests of the society by all possible means.

* Barruel's Memoirs, Vol III. Chap. 14.

A degree of superviforfhip and infpection is likewife committed to the Scotch Knights, and even to the Major and Minor Illuminees, over the Minerval, and other preparatory claffes, but at the fame time they themfelves are under the conftant infpection of Prefects and Regents, to whom alone the real views of the order are known.*

The inftructions given to thefe feveral agents of Illuminifm, would ferve greatly to unfold the art, and difcover the object, of the inftitution. They are a compound of whatever the higheft machivelian policy could fuggeft, to conceal, and yet advance the ends of the fubtle projector, and to acquire and maintain a tyrannical afcendency over the minds of men ; but they are too numerous to be introduced here.†

Very juft is the remark made by Profeffor Renner, one of the deponents on the fubject, *That the great ftrength of the order confifts in its invifibility.* A brother may know the fecrets of his clafs, and thofe of an inferior one, but all above him are entirely unknown ; unlefs his fuperiors have conferred on him the com-

---

* Barruel's Memoirs. Vol. III. Chap. 16.   † Ibid.
p. 175—242.

miſſion of Director, Viſitor, or Spy. The chiefs, by this method, watch an inferior, while they themſelves are concealed ; they know how far he is devoted to the order, and true to the ſecrets with which he is entruſted. If he has doubts, to whom can he reveal them with confidence, when the perſon to whom he commits himſelf, may be one employed to fift him, and who encourages his confidence only to betray him ?

" An advantage ſtill more important, reſults from this concealment, for ſhould any one be diſpoſed, he is incapable of diſcovering the ſu-ſuperiors of the order, while they at the ſame time can give their ſupport to any of the ac-cuſed without a ſuſpicion, perhaps, of being connected with them."

This inviſibility, as they call it, of the real Illuminees, it may be imagined excludes all communication from the lower to the ſuperior degrees ; whereas, in fact, any perſon belong-ing to the lower grades may exhibit a com-plaint againſt his Inſtructor, or aſk any privi-lege of the Provincial, National, or General, according to his ſtanding, while at the ſame time he remains wholly ignorant of the perſon he addreſſes, and even of the place of his reſi-

dence. Indeed, the inferiors of the order are
required to make, in this way, a monthly return to their invisible superiors, of the conduct
of those under their inspection, and of whatever they conceive materially interesting to
the institution.

This curious correspondence is conducted in
the following manner : A letter, with the direction of *Quibus Licet*, i. e. to whom it belongs, and marked with the sign of the class
of which the writer is a member, is opened
by the next superiors. Those having the addition of *Soli* or *Primo*, are conveyed to the
Provincial, National, or General, according to
the rank of the writer, and the direction
which is given, whether *Soli* or *Primo*.*

* Robison's Proofs, p. 177. Barruel's Memoirs, Vol.
III. p. 225. Vol. IV. p. 145 to 149.

C H A P. VIII.

The Discovery of the Sect.

THE firft alarm was given by a difcov-
ry of many dangerous publications which were
fecretly circulated; feveral of thefe were traced
back to the lodge Theodore, of which Weifhaupt was a member. Friendly remonftrances
were firft made by the Elector of Bavaria, on
the fubject, but thefe abufes continuing, he
ordered a judicial inquiry into the proceedings
of this lodge. It was found that this, and
feveral affociated lodges, were preparatory
fchools for another order of Mafons, who denominated themfelves

The Illuminated. Several called Minervals,
were faid to belong to this order, but the perfons, by whom they were admitted, were unknown. Some of thefe were privately examined by the Elector himfelf. They faid they
were bound to fecrecy; but they affured the

Elector, on their honor, that the aim of the order was useful both to church and state.

This not relieving the public anxiety, an order was published on the 22d of June, 1784, forbidding all secret assemblies, and shutting up the Mason lodges. The members of the lodge Theodore distinguished themselves by a pointed opposition to this order ; reprobating the prohibition as cruel, and continuing their meetings. By a subsequent edict, the order of the Illuminees was abolished, and search was made, in the lodge Theodore, for papers ; none of importance, however, were found.

In 1785, four Professors of the Marianen Academy, viz. Utschneider, Cosandey, Renner, and Grunberger, with some others, who appear to have withdrawn from the order, under a conviction of its evil tendency, were summoned before a court of inquiry. None of these had been admitted to the mysteries, yet their evidence was alarming. Their testimony agreed with what has been related respecting the lower degrees, and they further declared, " that, in the lodges, sensual pleasures were advocated, and self-murder justified, on epicurian and stoical principles ; that death was represented as an

eternal sleep; patriotism and loyalty were called narrow-minded prejudices, incompatible
with universal benevolence. Nothing was so
frequently discussed as the propriety of em-
ploying, for a good purpose, the means which
the wicked employed for evil purposes."

These depositions, given separately, under
oath, and the signature of the deponents, were
perfectly harmonious ; but the most offensive
parts were denied by the Illuminees, and much
clamor was raised. Weishaupt, however, was
deprived of his Professor's chair, and banished
from Bavaria. He went first to Regensburg,
and afterwards entered into the service of the
Duke of Saxe Gotha, whose name in the order was Timoleon.*

In 1786, a collection of original papers and
correspondence, was found in the house of
counsellor Zwack ; and soon after, a much
larger collection in the castle of Sanderdorf,
belonging to Baron Bassus. This collection
has been published, by order of the Elector,
under the title of " *Original Writings.*" From
these papers, principally, were taken the

* Robison's Proofs, p. 85 to 89. Barruel's Memoirs,
Vol IV. Chap. 7.

details respecting the code and government of
the Illuminees.* Some extracts from the epis-
tolary part of these writings will now be presented to the reader, more fully to bring into
view the object of the order, and the means
adopted to attain this object.

Spartacus, writing to Cato, on the subject of
establishing a peculiar morality and religion,
fitted for the great body of mankind, says,
" But this is a ticklish project, and requires
the utmost circumspection. The squeamish
will start at the sight of religious and political
novelties ; and they must be prepared for
them. We must be particularly careful about
the books we recommend. I shall confine
them at first to moralists, and reasoning histo-
rians. *Robinet, Mirabeau, the Social System, Natural Polity, the Philosophy of Nature,* and such
works are reserved for our higher degrees.
At present they must not even be mentioned
to our adepts, and particularly *Helvetius on
Man.*" The reader here sees a list of the most
anti-religious, atheistical productions, and that
they are reserved for the last mysteries. " Marius," he adds, " an excellent man, must be
dealt with. His stomach, which cannot yet

* Robison's Proofs, p. 107.   Barruel's Memoirs, Vol.
III. p. 145

digeft fuch ftrong food, muft acquire a better
tone."* But after all the cautious fteps of
the leader, Knigge, in a letter to Zwack, expreffes his apprehenfions, that "*fuch a fupera-
bundance of atheifm would betray the tendency of the
fect too foon.*"†

Brutus writes, "Numenius (Count Kollow-
rath) now acquiefces in the mortality of the
foul, but, I fear we fhall lofe Ludovicus Bava-
rus. He told Spartacus that he was miftaken
when he thought that he had fwallowed his
ftupid Mafonry."‡

Weifhaupt, writing to Cato, an account of
his degree of priefts, fays, "One would almoft imagine, that this degree, as I have man-
aged it, is real Chriftianity. In this fenfe,
no man need be afhamed of being a Chriftian, for I preferve the name, and fubftitute
reafon."§

* Robifon's Proofs, p. 109. Barruel's Memoirs, Vol.
IV. p. 43.

† Barruel's Memoirs, Vol. IV. Obfervations, p. 8.

‡ Robifon's Proofs, p. 169.

§ Robifon's Proofs, p. 119. Barruel's Memoirs, Vol.
III. p. 144.

The Areopagites, though united in their object, appear to have differed much with reſpect
to the beſt means of attaining it ; while ſome
were fearful of alarming the adepts by too
haſty diſcoveries, others were diſguſted with
the tedious ſlowneſs of this proceſs of deceit.
Minos (Baron Dittfurt) " wanted to introduce atheiſm at once, and not go hedging in
the manner they did ; affirming, it was eaſier
to ſhow at once that atheiſin was friendly to
ſociety, than to explain all their maſonic
Chriſtianity, which they were afterwards to
ſhow to be *a bundle of lies*."* Language cannot
furniſh a phraſe, more deſcriptive than this, of
the nature of Illuminiſm; the whole ſyſtem was
"a bundle of lies," a plan of concealed falſehood
and deception. The means perfectly correſ-
pond with the deſign of the projectors, and
ſufficiently explain the nature of that deſign.

We have before been led to notice the importance which theſe conſpirators attribute to
ſecret ſocieties, as the main ſpring of their deſtructive machinery. While they are perpetually reminding each other, that here lay their
hopes of ſucceſs, it becomes us not to loſe
ſight of this engine of miſchief. The following is an extract from a lecture, which Wei-

* Robiſou's Proofs, p. 135.

fhaupt read to his adepts on this fubject.
" When the object is an univerfal revolution,
all the members of thefe focieties muſt find
means of governing invifibly, and without
any appearance of violence, men of all ſtations,
of all nations, and of every religion. Infinuate
the fame fpirit every where. In filence, but
with the greateſt activity poſſible, direct thefcat-
tered inhabitants of the earth toward the fame
point." In proof of the importance of fuch a
fecret union, he reafons thus : " The flighteſt
obfervation fhews that nothing will fo much
contribute to increafe the zeal of the members
as fecret union. We fee with what keennefs
and zeal the frivolous bufinefs of Free Mafonry is conducted by perfons knit together by
the fecrecy of their union."*

Among their plans of deception was found
a fcheme " for a public literary academy, to
confiſt of two claffes of men ; the one of men
remarkable for their zeal in religion, the other
of profound Illuminees. Each member to
wear on his breaſt a medal with this infcrip-
tion, *Religioni et Scientiis*," (to religion and

L

fciences.)* " *And no marvel ; for Satan himfelf is transformed into an angel of light.*"

Spartacus, writing to Cato, fays, " There muft not a fingle purpofe come in fight that is ambiguous, and that may betray our aims againft religion and the ftate. That we may be uncontroled in our difcourfe, let our pu-pils remark that the fuperiors enjoy great lat-itude in that refpect ; *that we fometimes fpeak in one way, and fometimes in another*, only to found the opinions of thofe we converfe with." This the pupil is told ; but he is not told that the real defign is, to fecure a retreat, when they have incautiously gone too far ; and to render their real fentiments impenetrable to their inferiors."†

Among the inftructions which Weifhaupt gives his difciples, " he exhorts, and ferioufly admonifhes thofe who have the care of rare books or precious manufcripts, in the libraries of princes, nobles, and religious orders, to take them for the benefit of thofe to whom they would be more ufeful." Sending a lift of what he would have taken from the libra-

* Barruel's Memoirs, Vol. IV. Obfervation, p. 9.

† Ibid Vol. III. p. 177. Robifon's Proofs, p. 119.

ry of the Carmes, he fays, " *all thofe would be of much greater ufe if they were in our hands. What do thofe rafcals do with all thofe books ?*"

Writing to Cato on the fame fubject he fays, " Marius (keeper of the archives of the Electorate) has ferreted out a noble document, which we have got. He makes it, forfooth, a cafe of confcience. How filly that ; fince only that is *fin*, which is *ultimately* productive of mifchief. In this cafe, where the advantage far exceeds the difadvantage, it is *meritorious virtue.*"*

But not fatisfied with robbing mankind of their money and books, he contrived as unjuftly to pilfer their fame, and appropriate to his order, their deferved reputation. At one time his direction is, " to endeavor to gain, or ruin every rifing character." At another, he gives the Regents the following inftructions ; " It is very proper to make your inferiors believe, without telling them the real ftate of the cafe, that all other fecret focieties, particularly that of Free Mafonry, are fecretly directed by us. Or elfe, and it is really the fact in fome ftates, that potent *monarchs* are governed by our order. When any thing re-

* Robifon's Proofs, p. 110. Barruel's Memoirs, Vol. III. p. 57.

markable or important comes to pass, hint that it originated with our order. *Should any person by his merit acquire a great reputation, let it be generally understood that he is one of us.*"*

There was found in the hand writing of Zwack, a project for a fisterhood. It contains the following passages. " It will be of great service, and procure us much information and money, and will suit charmingly many of our truest members, who are lovers of the sex. It should consist of two classes, the virtuous, and the freer hearted ; they must not know each other, and must be under the direction of men, but without knowing it. Proper books must be put into their hands, and such (but secretly) as are flattering to their passions."

A list and description of eighty five young ladies of Manheim, was found with this project. Minos makes an offer of his wife, and his four daughters in law to be the first adepts. " The eldest," he says, " is excellent. She is twenty four, has read much, is above all prejudices, *and in religion, thinks as I do.*"

It appears that the institution of a lodge was attempted at Frankfort, and a discourse, as delicate as the fentiments of fuch men could conceive, was prepared for the occafion. After much of the tortuous eloquence of Illuminifm, the orator thus addreffes his fair affembly. " Rejoice in the dawn of Illumination and freedom. Nature at laft enjoys her facred never fading rights. Long was her voice kept down by civil fubordination ; but the days of your majority now draw nigh, and you will no longer, under the authority of guardians, account it a reproach to confider with enlightened eyes the fecret work fhops of nature, and to enjoy your work and duty." Minos thought this very fine, but it raifed a terrible difturbance, and broke up the affembly.*

Among thefe papers was likewife found the defcription of a ftrong box, which, if forced open, would blow up and deftroy the contents ; feveral receipts for procuring abortion ; a compofition which blinds or kills when thrown in the face ; a method for filling a bed chamber with peftilential vapors ; the fecret of taking off and imitating the impreffions of feals, fo as to ufe them afterwards ; a collec-

L 2

tion of one hundred and thirty seals of princes, nobles, clergymen, merchants, &c. a re-
ceipt ad excitandum furorem uterinam ; a
manuscript entitled, " Better than Horus,"
which contained all the blasphemies of atheism ; a dissertation on suicide : also injunctions
to all the superiors to learn to write with both
hands ; and that they should use more than
one cypher.

The reader, perhaps, will find it difficult to
conceive how this horrid artillery could be
made conducive to the ends which the order
professed to have in view, the advancement
of religion, and social good. The Illuminees
have furnished us with a solution. " This
apparatus, they said, was with propriety in
the hands of counsellor Zwack who was a
judge of a criminal court, and whose duty it
was to know such things." Admitting this,
one thing still remains unaccounted for, viz.
how they come to be put with the papers of
the Illuminees ?*

In consequence of these discoveries, some
were deposed from offices they sustained, and
several banished. Apologies, and partial rep-

* Robison's Proofs, p. 111, 112.   Barruel's Memoirs,
Vol. IV. p. 167.

refentations of Illuminifm were publifhed, and great was the outcry of cruelty which refounded from all quarters ; while others, imputed the lenity of government on this occa- fion, to the invifible influence which the order had gained over the meafures of the court.*

It appears that Illuminifm had made a prog- refs proportionate to the zeal of the actors ; Bavaria alone is faid to have contained about fix hundred. Three of the witnefles above mentioned declare, " that while connected with the order, they were feveral times in- formed that it had extended to Italy, to Ven- ice, to Auftria, to Holland, Saxony on the Rhine, and even to *America*." In the original writings feveral lodges in *America* are put on the lift. This was before 1786.

A report refpecting the progrefs of the or- der in Greece (Bavaria,) was found among the papers of Zwack, in his hand writing, which prefents an alarming view of the prev- alence of Illuminifm, at a time when the public fcarcely knew that the order was in exiftence. After mentioning a number of lodges, under the direction of the Illuminees,

* Barruel's Memoirs, Vol. IV. Chap. 8.

in feveral parts of the electorate, it is noted, " At Munich we have bought an houfe, and have taken our meafures fo well, that they even fpeak of us with efteem. This is a great deal for this city. We have a good mufeum of natural hiftory, and apparatus for experiments. The garden is well occupied by botanic fpecimens, and the whole has the appearance of a fociety of zealous naturalifts."

" The Dowager Duchefs has fet up her academy entirely according to our plan. All the Profeffors are of *our order*, and all the pupils will be ours."

" On the recommendation of the brethren, *Pylades* is made the *ecclefiaftical fifcal councellor*, and has the church money at his difpofal. By properly ufing this money, we have already repaired the mal-adminiftration of ——, and of ——, and have affifted more brethren under fimilar misfortunes."

" The brethren who are in orders have all been provided with livings and curacies, or with preceptor's places."

" All the German fchools, and the benevolent focieties, are all left or

"We fhall fhortly be mafters of the
Bartholomew inftitution for the education of
*young ecclefiatics. By this means we fhall be able
to flock all Bavaria with priefts both clever and
proper.*"

"We have at length got the remaining
revenues of the Jefuits under the control
of the order. This coft our fenate fome
nights want of fleep."*

This difcovery very much difconcerted the
plans of the Illuminees, but it did not alter
their habits or principles. Under a new name,
and with new agents, we fhall find them, in
the following chapter, purfuing the fame object, and we fhall fee the long train which infidelity has been preparing, kindled into an
explofion which has changed the face of Europe, and been felt by remote nations.

He who habituates his mind to ferious re-
flections, and is fuitably difpofed to derive inftruction from the fcenes around him, will
find means of improvement, even among thefe
difgufting objects. He will at leaft, feel his

* Robifon's Proofs, p. 155—159. Barruel's Memoirs,
Vol. IV. p. 161, 57—59.

inactivity in a worthy caufe reproved, by the labors, the zeal, the unremitting perfeverance of thefe agents of deftruction ; for who can boaft an equal engagednefs, a mind equally awake to feize every opportunity and advantage, for promoting the caufe of religion and the good of fociety, with what thefe men difcover, in laboring for the deftruction of both ?

C H A P. IX.

The GERMAN UNION.

A NOTE, tranfmitted from Germany to England, appeared in the Monthly Magazine of January, 1798 ; in which the public were affured, " that from the beginning of the year 1790, every concern of the Illuminati has ceafed, and no lodge of Free Mafons in Germany, has, fince that period, taken the leaft notice of them."* It is worthy of remark, that this certificate implicitly acknowledges, that until 1790, the Illuminees did exift, and were connected with the lodges of Free Mafons in Germany ; yet thofe, who endeavored to convince the public of their exiftence, at the time in which it is here acknowledged, were as contemptuoufly fcouted, as thofe are, who now believe the fubject important to mankind.

* Barruel's Memoirs, Vol. IV. p. 180.

But are such men as Weishaupt and his
coadjutors, thus easily beat off from their
purposes ? Do such Ethiopians so readily
change their skin ? No, Weishaupt himself,
has sufficiently, though unintentionally, warned us not to depend on such declarations.
Writing to Cato, he says, "I have foreseen
every thing ; I have prepared every thing.
Let my whole order go to rack and ruin ; in
three years I will answer to restore it, and
that to a more powerful state than it was
in before. Obstacles only stimulate my
activity."[*]

How far he was active, after his banish-
ment, in promoting the cause of Illuminism,
does not appear, but a new confederation, on
similar principles, and pursuing the same object, was formed, called the *German Union*. It
was expedient that known Illuminees should
take a less active part in this new arrangement. Probably the advice which was found
in the hand writing of Cato, was adopted on
this occasion, which was this : " In order to
re-establish our affairs, let some of the ablest of
those brethren, who have avoided our misfortunes, take the place of our founders."[†]

* Barruel's Memoirs, Vol. IV. p. 130.   † Ibid, p. 178.

The Illuminees, in projecting this fecond part, appear to have taken their clue from the following exifting circumftances. That fcheme of religion, which excludes from the gofpel all its *peculiarities*, had, for fome time, been making a rapid progrefs in Germany. One excefs led on to another, till doctrines were advanced among the clergy, which would leave the fuperiority of Chriftianity, to natural religion, very doubtful. This tendency to infidelity, appears to have been, in a great degree, owing to the influence of the Anti-Chriftian confpiracies, of which we have been fpeaking ; but, however this may be, it was found to be a very convenient ftock on which to ingraft a branch of Illuminifm. An opportunity was now given, to fuch as wifhed to extirpate Chriftianity, to take part with thofe divines who were ftriving to explain away its diftinguifhing doctrines.

On thefe circumftances was founded the idea of the German Union. A multitude of writers appeared who exprefied great zeal for Chriftianity ; but the manifeft object of this zeal was, to reduce it to a fyftem of natural religion. The Bible was explained, corrected, allegorized, and otherwife twifted, till the minds of men had hardly any thing left

M

to reft on, as a doctrine of revealed religion. This was a fignal for others to come forward, deny revelation, and affert that man had no other ground of confidence than the dictates of natural reafon. Another fet of writers, proceeding from this as a point already fettled, profcribed all religion whatever, and openly taught the doctrines of materialifm and atheifm.* But it afterwards appeared, that thefe movements were the effects of combination and defign, and that an affociation was formed who were unitedly ftriving to drive things to this extremity.

One Barth, a doctor of divinity in the univerfity at Halle, was the principal agent in this combination. He was an Illuminee, and a perfon of moft infamous morals. In this inftance Mr. Ebeling acknowledges, that, "As to Barth, Robifon is not very erroneous." But, even here, he appears much difpofed to palliate, and tells us that " Barth did not write againft religion ; but only attempted to *modernife Chriftianity.*" He even feems to recommend his writings, from this confideration, that " He knew vice by *experience*, and could fhew all its

_____
* Robifon's Proofs, p. 66 to 72. Barruel's Memoirs, Vol. IV. p. 192 to 194.

deformity." Yet even Mr. Ebeling does not
pretend that he ever ceased to love vice, or to
practice it.

The dissoluteness of his morals had deprived him of the means of a decent subsistence,
when, on a sudden, he purchased, near Halle, a
large mansion, which he called Earth's ruhe.
This became the head quarters of the Union.
The management of this institution was committed to twenty two conductors, whose
agents were dispersed through the different
towns. The persons chiefly sought after, were
authors, post masters, printers, and booksellers.
While every encouragement was given to
those works which favored their designs, it
was found difficult, in some instances, to procure the publication of works designed to correct these evils. Every obstruction was given
to the circulation of those of this description,
which had come from the press ; and funds
were to be established to indemnify those
booksellers, who, instead of selling such
books, would conceal them in their shops.

But the principal means, on which they depended for corrupting the public mind, were
literary societies, or *reading clubs ;* which they
labored to set up in every town. These were

modifications of Weifhaupt's minerval fchools, they became very numerous ; and it was the bufinefs of the fecretaries, and initiated book-fellers, to have them furnifhed with books of the moft Anti-Chriftian character.

One of the vileft things, publifhed on this occafion, was, the " Edict for Religion," written in derifion of fome regulations, publifhed by the king of Pruffia, under that title. This was traced to Barth's ruhe. He was there-upon arrefted, his papers feized, and he imprifoned. This put a ftop to the bufinefs of the Union ; but Dr. Robifon quotes perfons *in high office at Berlin*, as agreeing in opinion, that the affociation of writers, and other turbulent perfons in Germany, has been but very faintly hit by this blow, and is almoft as active as ever.*

As Mr. Ebeling fpeaks in the moft contemptuous manner, of Dr. Robifon's *perfons in high office at Berlin*, I beg leave to introduce here, the fentiments of fome of that court upon the fubject, and in particular, thofe of the king of Pruffia, whom Mr. Ebeling mentions in the higheft terms of refpect, and ranks with the beft of princes.

* Proofs, p. 221 to 245. Memoirs, Vol. IV. p. 195 to 204

The Chevalier Von Hamelberg, a major in the king of Pruſſia's ſervice, lately tranſlated Dr. Robiſon's work into the German language, and preſented a copy of the work to his ſovereign, to which the king made the following return :

" *My dear Major Hamelberg,*

" The work which you have tranſlated and communicated to me, with your letter of March 3d, expoſes the pernicious tendency of all ſecret ſocieties in the cleareſt light, and is entitled to a conſiderable degree of merit with your countrymen. I, therefore, moſt willingly expreſs my warmeſt ſatisfaction, and moſt ſincere thanks, for the copy which has been tranſmitted to me, and I hereby announce my approbation of the work, as your affectionate king, FREDERICK WILLIAM."

CHARLOTTENBURG, *July* 25, 1800.

This was communicated to Dr. Robiſon, in a letter from major Hamelberg. This letter is ſo well calculated to throw light upon this ſubject, that I cannot refrain from introducing the more intereſting parts of it.

" Sir,

"I have at last, after a long search, succeeded in my endeavors to obtain your valuable work on the secret societies, which was so thoroughly suppressed in *Germany*, that it was not possible to procure a copy of. As soon as I obtained it, I communicated it to some friends, as much distinguished by their character as by their talents; who, being all convinced of its excellence, persuaded me to translate it into German. As the whole merit of the work is yours, sir, I feel it to be my duty to send you the enclosed answer from the king my master. And should you be of opinion that it will serve the good cause, you are at liberty to make any use of it which you may think proper. I think it necessary, sir, to apprize you that I have added some notes, and some facts which have come within my knowledge, and which evidently prove (were any further proof required) *both the truth of your assertions, and the reality of the dangers* to which the sovereigns, as well as the regular governments, are exposed wherever these societies are tolerated. I beg you will be convinced, sir, of the distinguished consideration with which I have the honor to be, sir, yours, &c.

VON HAMELBERG."

Minden, *(Westphalia) July* 27, 1800.

The preceding letters were communicated by Dr. Robison to the editors of the Anti-Jacobin Review, and from that copied in the New England Palladium, of May 29, 1801.

These letters came attended with an anecdote, which, though not supported by equal vouchers, yet so perfectly accords with the practices of the German Union, and so satisfactorily accounts for the scarcity of Robison's work in Germany, as induces me to give it a place in the conclusion of this chapter.

" Gofchen, a bookseller at Leipzig, had engaged a person to make a hasty translation of Professor Robison's book, and nearly a dozen sheets had been printed, when an Englishman, who spoke German with all the purity and fluency of a native, came to his house, and telling him, that he had himself already translated the work, and that it would appear within a week, persuaded Gofchen to sell him his edition, for a handsome price, which was immediately paid. By this means Gofchen's translation was suppressed, and the other never appeared. The same thing, we have been assured, occurred at Berlin."

C H A P. X.

The FRENCH REVOLUTION.

IF the tendency of those principles which we have seen originating in France, and communicated from thence to the German lodges, is not already apparent, we have a fair experiment before us, which fully discovers their nature. We have the fruits, to enable us to judge of the qualities of the tree. It has been observed, that the French lodges, already the nurseries of every infidel and licentious sentiment, had communicated to their German brethren those doctrines, which the wicked ingenuity of Weishaupt had wrought up into that systematical process of corruption, comprised in Illuminism.

While these things were transacting in Germany, the same principles were spreading, gaining strength, and tending to an explosion in France. The French lodges had become schools, not for promoting revolutionary opinions merely, but for training men to that

hardinefs in iniquity, that familiarity with
blood and flaughter, that crafement of every
natural affeftion, and fentiment of tendernefs,
which prepare men to plunge the poignard into a brother's breaft. How well thefe mafonic
fchools were adapted to prepare men for fuch
fcenes as have been exhibited in France, may
be perceived from the following ceremony
ufed in the Grand Orient.

" A candidate for reception into one of the
higheft orders, after having heard many
threatenings denounced againft all who fhould
betray the fecrets of the order, was conducted
to a place where he faw the dead bodies of
feveral who were faid to have fuffered for
their treachery. He then faw his own brother
tied hand and foot, begging his mercy and
interceffion. He was informed that this perfon was about to fuffer the punifhment due for
this offence, and that it was referved for him
(the candidate) to be the inftrument of this
juft vengeance, and that this gave him an opportunity of manifefting that he was completely devoted to the order. It being ob-
ferved that his countenance gave figns of in-
ward horror (the perfon in bonds imploring
his mercy all the while) he was told, that in
order to fpare his feelings, a bandage fhould

be put over his eyes. A dagger was then put into his right hand, and being hoodwinked, his left hand was laid on the palpitating heart of the criminal, and he was then ordered to ftrike. He inftantly obeyed ; and when the bandage was taken from his eyes, he faw that it was a lamb he had ftabbed."*

Many of the French lodges needed not to be inftructed in Weifhaupt's theories, to qualify them for the higheft degrees of Illuminifm. The inftructions of Voltaire had fufficiently difpoffefled them of what, in the language of modern philofophy, is called *prejudice* and *fu-perftition,* i. e. every fentiment of religious or moral obligation ; but a fyftem, and a regular fubordination and correfpondence, were wanting to give thefe principles their full force.

In this ftate of things, Mirabeau returned from Germany, highly illuminated; and, at his requeft, two of the German Areopagites, viz. Bode, and Baron de Bufche, met him in France, in 1788, to form the French lodges into a duly organized body. Their bufinefs was eafily tranfacted. Before the end of March, 1789, the whole of the Grand Orient, confift-

* Robifon's Proofs. p. 220.

ing of 266 lodges, had the fecrets of Illumination communicated to them.* By the means
of fecret committees every part of this extenfive body was in a ftate of clofe connection
and correfpondence ; and it was in the power
of the prime movers of this machine to direct
the force of the whole to any point.†

It is not, however, to be underftood that
every member of this body entered into the
views of the profound Illuminees. The Duke
of Orleans himfelf, the Grand Mafter of thefe
lodges, deceived by the confpirators with the
vain hope of afcending the throne of France,
was but the tool of their defigns.

Under the direction of the German deputies,
a club was formed at Verfailles, compofed of
the moft profound adepts, called the *Breton
Club.* This fociety, by means of its committees in all the illuminated lodges, obtained a
moft powerful influence in the affairs of the
nation. The members of this club, compofed
the leaders of a club, which afterwards met
at the *Convent of Jacobins* in Paris, and from

* Robifon's Proofs, p. 287, 303—307. Barruel's Memoirs, Vol. IV. p. 210—213.

† Ibid. p. 307 ; and Vol. II. p. 239.

that circumstance, was denominated the *Jacobin Club.* The proceedings of the National
Convention were entirely subject to the influence of this usurping confederacy ; and by
their secret agents, and committees they inflamed the minds of the populace, and directed
their blind rage at pleasure. It was the atrocious measures of these banditti which gave
to the French revolution its peculiarly horrid
features, and has attached perpetual infamy to
the term *Jacobin.**

As a great variety of circumstances, too
many to be introduced into this work, and
which cannot be abridged without weakening
their force, are adduced by Barruel, in proof
of the influence of this illuminated society in

* It is really a cause of pain to the author, that he
finds himself necessitated to introduce a term in a very
odious sense. which is used to distinguish the particular
political opinions of some of his countrymen, whom,
whatever names they may bear, he regards as friends to
religion, to order, and good government ; and he now
gives notice that the term *Jacobin*, as here used, is to be
considered as applied, not to those who are innocently misled, but to those only who neither *fear God*, nor *regard
man.*

Robison's Proofs, p. 311, 376.   Barruel's Memoirs,
Vol. IV. Chap. 11 and 12.

directing the revolution ; I beg leave to adduce fome evidence of this fact from another
quarter.

That judicious and accurate obferver, John
Moore, M. D. was, at the period of which we
are fpeaking, occafionally in Paris, and frequently attended at the national affembly, and
at the Jacobin club, and though then ignorant of the fyftematical combination which
guided the revolution, yet remarked, that
" moft queftions of great importance are dif-
cuffed in the Jacobin fociety of Paris, before
they are introduced into the national affembly;
and the fuccefs they are likely to have in the
fecond, may be generally known by that
which they have in the firft. Societies of the
fame name and nature are eftablifhed all over
France, which hold a regular correfpondence
with the parent fociety at Paris, and by mu-
tually communicating information and advice, act with wonderful eficacy on important occafions."

He alfo quotes, with approbation, a letter
from M. la Fayette, of June 16, 1792, who
then perceived that he had been kept ignorant
of the real views of fome whom he had confidered as the friends of a juft and equal lib-

N

erty. His expressions are, " The Jacobin faction has produced all the diforders ; it is that
fociety which I loudly accufe of it. Organized like a feparate empire, and blindly governed by fome ambitious men, this fociety
forms a diftinct corporation in the middle of
the French nation, whofe power it ufurps,
and whofe reprefentatives it fubdues." This
letter proved the ruin of the Marquis.*

The American Revolution doubtlefs haftened
the final cataftrophe of affairs in France. The
French officers and foldiers, by the new ideas
which they had acquired in America, of liberty and the rights of man, were prepared to
efpoufe this caufe in their own country. It
is obvious, however, that the aim of the
leaders in France was not to deftroy the
power which oppreffed the nation, but to
transfer that power into their own hands.
Fayette and his companions became tools of
their ambitious defigns ; and, when they had
acted the parts affigned them, were facrificed.
Nothing was further from the views of the
French nation, at the beginning of the revolution, than what has taken place. The object
held up to them was perpetually varying.

* Moore's Jour. Vol. I. p. 67—70.   Bofton edi. 1794.

They were firft illuminated, literally blind-
folded and wheedled, till by bribes, by threatenings, and by having their paffions inflamed
by falfe reprefentations, they were prepared
to follow their leaders.

How different were the circumftances attending the American revolution ? Here the
object in view was clear and definite. The
public will was one, and that will was faithfully executed. Accordingly, thofe who firft
ftood forth the defenders of their country's rights, acquired an influence, a reputation, and an intereft in the public confidence,
which furmounted all oppofition, and which
remained, unimpaired, during the whole revolution.

The caufe of this diffimilarity, in the two
revolutions, is evident. In America, the
ftruggle was the refult of a genuine fpirit of
freedom, feeking the protection of its rights,
in equal laws ; in France, it was the refult of
a faction, facrificing to its deteftable views
the moft facred rights of man, and crufhing
all who oppofed its ambitious defigns. The
friends of moderation, of juftice, and a rational liberty, when they ceafed to fecond the
views of the confpirators were profcribed,

and the illuminated chiefs, by means of the
masonic lodges, governed the nation.

Dr. Robison, on the authority of Mr. Le-
franc, President of the seminary of the Eudists
at Caen, in Normandy, and of Mr. Latocnaye,
an emigrant gentleman, represents France as
a vast masonic combination, directed by secret
influence. In proof of this it is observed,
" that all the irreligious and seditious doctrines of the day, and the enthusiastic principles by which the public mind was, as it were,
set on fire, were the subjects of perpetual har-
angues in the Mason lodges ; that the distribution of France into departments, districts,
circles, cantons, &c. is perfectly similar, and
with the same denominations, to a distribution
which he had remarked in the correspondence
of the Grand Orient ; that the President's
hat, in the national assembly, is copied from
that of a Grand Master ; that the scarf of a
municipal officer is the same with that of a
brother apprentice ; that when the assembly
celebrated the revolution in the cathedral,
they accepted of the highest honors of Masonry, by passing under an *arch of steel*, formed
by the drawn swords of two ranks of brethren, and that the national assembly protected the

meetings of Free Masons, while it peremptorily prohibited every other private meeting."*

It was a discovery of the horrid designs of these conductors of the French revolution, and not, as some pretend, a dereliction of the principles of liberty, which has alienated the virtuous part of our countrymen from their attachment to the cause of France. When it was announced in America, that millions of Frenchmen were striving for freedom, who did not bestow a benediction on their cause, and fervently pray for its success? The triumphs of France were celebrated here with real joy, and her misfortunes were lamented as our own. Long did we strive to palliate her crimes, and long did we invent excuses for her enormities. But when at length the mask fell off, and we saw in the boasted friend of his country the disgusting atheist, the factious leader, the man who could smile at carnage, and feast on havock and war, our feelings revolted; we could no longer receive as brethren, men who proved themselves the enemies of religion, of order, of humanity.

N 2

* Robison's Proofs, p. 294—298.

The co-operation of the Illuminees of other nations, and their joint exertions to extend the revolution, prove that it was the work of that order ; and that France was no less indebted to her secret agents than to her martial prowess, for the unexampled success of her arms.

At the commencement of the revolution, a manifesto was sent from the grand national lodge of Free Masons, (so it is entitled) at Paris, signed by the Duke of Orleans, as Grand Master, addressed to the lodges in all the respectable cities of Europe, exhorting them to unite for the support of the French revolution, and to kindle a spirit of revolution through all lands ; some of these were addressed to those, of whose assistance they were assured, and to such were given earnest exhortations to *establish, in every quarter, secret schools of political education ; and schools for the education of children, under the direction of well disciplined masters ; and offers of pecuniary assistance for this purpose, and for the encouragement of writers in favor of the revolution, and for patriotic booksellers, who suffer by their endeavours to suppress publications which have an opposite tendency.* All this is genuine Illuminism, and may help us to account for the mysterious scarcity of Dr. Robison's work in Germany.*

* See page 158.

Among many other foreign lodges, the grand national lodge at Paris, had the particular direction of a club, in the form of a mafonic lodge, called *Propaganda*, which met weekly, and had its agents and emiffaries in all parts of Europe.

Thefe facts are collected from a Hamburg Journal, for 1790, and from a publication of Profeffor Hoffman, whom the Illuminees had long ftriven to gain to their interefts, and who was employed by the more refpectable Mafons, to make public thefe machinations of the occult lodges. The refult of his inquiries was, " that the Propaganda works in every corner to this hour, and its emiffaries run about in all the four quarters of the globe, and are to be found in numbers in every city that is a feat of government."*

Thefe invifible agents were by no means idle or unfuccefsful. There is reafon to believe that France was much indebted to them for their progrefs in Germany, Holland, Italy, and other parts. The proofs brought in fupport of thefe facts are too much involved with circumftances to find a place here.

* Robifon's Proofs, p. 315—319. Barruel's Memoirs, Vol. IV. p. 283, 306.

One curious inftance, however, related in a book called Paragraphen ; in another performance, with the title of Cri de la Raifon ; and in a third, called Les Mafques arrachées, muft not be omitted. The inftance referred. to, is the following.

Cuftine was accufed before the revolutionary tribunal of treachery, by Zimmerman, for refufing the offer of Manheim, when he himfelf engaged to deliver it into his hands. Cuftine's anfwer is remarkable. " Hardly," faid he, " had I fet my foot in Germany, when this man, and all the fools of his country, befieged me, and would have delivered up to me their towns and villages. What occafion had I to do any thing to Manheim, when the prince was neutral ?"*

Thefe fecret agents of Illuminifm, appear to have had another object attached to their miffion, viz. the removal of thofe who ftood much in the way of the revolution. When it was underftood that Guftavus III, king of Sweden, was to command the confederate armies, Ankerftroem, by the expeditious procefs of aſſaſſination, relieved the Jacobins from their fears, and in recompence they honor him with a ſtatue.*

When the expected union of the emperor of Germany and the king of Pruſſia, alarmed the Jacobins, the following *comfortable* re-flections were annexed to the account in a Straſburgh Journal, No. 53. "*In thoſe coun-tries, where the fate of ſeveral millions of men, hangs on a bit of paſte, or on the rupture of a little vein, one can calculate on nothing. A ſingle indigeſtion, or a drop of blood forced from its proper veſſels, will be ſufficient to diſſolve this brilliant union.*" This comment on the expected union was dated from Vienna, the 26th of February, 1792. Leo-pold died (poiſoned) on the 1ſt of March following.†

On the ſucceeding Auguſt, it was motion-ed in the national aſſembly, " To levy a body of twelve hundred patriotic volunteers, by a penſion of two thouſand livers yearly, with a reverſion to their children to the third gener-ation ; whoſe buſineſs it ſhould be to aſſaſſin-

* Barruel's Memoirs, Vol. I. p. 123. † Ibid. Vol. IV. p. 308. Travels of two Frenchmen in the North, Vol. V. Chap. 12.

ate the generals and princes who commanded
the armies which attacked France.   An ap-
prehenſion of repriſals prevented the adoption
of the propoſal."   Mr. Moore in his account of
this buſineſs, adds this circumſtance, " That
though it did not paſs in the aſſembly, it
was by them ſent to the commiſſion extra-
ordinaire."*

The fate of the emperor taught his young
ſucceſſor more caution.   His firſt care was to
diſmiſs all the Italian cooks, that he might not
become a victim to what was called the *Naples
broth*.†   The Illuminee, who believes all means
lawful for the attainment of a good end, can
feel no remorſe for ſuch deeds of darkneſs ;
but, for the honor of modern times, it is de-
ſirable that our hiſtory ſhould not be ſtained
with many ſimilar facts.

* Moore's Journal, Boſton edit. 1794. Vol. I. p.
128—131.

† Barruel's Memoirs, Vol. IV. p. 308.   Robiſon's
Proofs, p. 311.

C H A P. XI.

A Summary View of Illuminism.

THESE are the leading features of that ſyſtem of deception in which we ſee the ene-mies of religion quitting the open field of ar-gument, in which they have ſo often been defeated, and flying to the arts of ſophiſtry, corruption, and concealment. But it is not from a curſory glance that we can acquire a juſt idea of the depths of that wicked ſubtlety compriſed in Illuminiſm. Let us take a view of this deſtructive engine in a more compact operation.

Imagine an illuminated Inſinuator attack-ing a youth of talents and principle, in whom the moral ſenſe of right and wrong is yet vigorous ; for it is for the ſeduction of ſuch, more particularly, that the artful proceſs of Illumination is deſigned. From this Inſinua-tor he hears, as by accident, however, that theſe are ſchools of wiſdom, ſeats of ſcience, in which the wife and good are uniting for the important end of secretly ruling mankind, and thus delivering them from those calamities, for which all other means are found to be ineffectual. If, by such suggestions, he is led to express a desire to become a member of this society, the Insinuator promises his utmost assistance ; but he is told, that this is the reward only of long approved merit.

To excite his curiosity, it is intimated, that there exist doctrines solely transmitted by secret traditions, because they are above the comprehension of common minds ; and letters, filled with mysterious characters, are, as it were incautiously, exposed to his view. To increase his ardor to become a member, the Insinuator expatiates frequently on the supreme pleasure of secretly reigning ; and remarks, that it is easy for one man of parts to lead thousands, if he but knew his own advantages. That he may be led to consider the interests of the order as his own, he is told of its readiness and power to protect him, and secure his success in all the pursuits of life. Questions of the most ensnaring nature are proposed to discover his sentiments, and books, secretly conveying the poison of infidelity, are made use of to corrupt them. If he discovers a weak part, it is noted for a point of attack. If he expresses a doubt respecting any of the important principles of religion and morality, he is sure of being applauded for his strength of mind in rising above the prejudices of education, which he is often told, are the sources of all our errors. He is placed in situations where he hears the most artful sophistry used to prove, that patriotism and private affections are narrow minded prejudices; that the bonds of marriage and parental authority are encroachments on the natural rights of man; that suicide is lawful; that sensual pleasures correspond with the law of nature, and that it is proper to employ, for a good purpose, those means which wicked men use for evil purposes.

While every art is thus employed to undermine the principles of morality and religion, his fears are lulled by constant declamations on the excellence of virtue, and the highly honorable, and most useful and benevolent intentions of the superiors of the order. It is one of the prime arts of Illuminism to extol the name of virtue, in general, and at the same time, to sap its foundation in every particular. The object is continually varying, and the mind, led by new invented systems and

O

explanations, in a thousand different directions, is, at length, totally bewildered, and all clear distinction between truth and error is lost. How can the unwary youth escape these snares so artfully spread, and sufficient, indeed, *" if it were possible, to deceive the very elect ?"*

And what could have been the design of this subtle process of deception, of all these studied phrases, and nicely adjusted degrees ? Were they designed merely to discover the ingenuity of the contriver ? Or, did he who contrived them, in fact, contemplate some great revolution, which rendered the introduction of all this machinery necessary ? The latter is not denied by those who most zealously advocate the innocence of Illuminism. They were intended, they acknowledge, to demolish the strong holds of superstition and despotism. But when the mind is dispossessed of all that these terms imply, in the language of Illuminism, what remains ? What religious principle, moral sentiment, or social affection, can exist in that heart which has been the subject of this truly diabolical renovation ?

Were this question proposed to an Illuminee, his answer doubtless would be, What can exist ? The noblest of all affections, the fum of all virtue, *Cofmopolitifm.* Far from difcarding virtue, we only are her true worfhippers, who erect her temple, not on the narrow foundation of private affection, but on the broad bafis of univerfal love.

As this term comprifes every thing of duty and moral obligation to which the Illuminee makes any pretenfions, it becomes neceffary, in order to our forming a judgment of that fyftem, that this boafted virtue fhould pafs a more particular examination.

A Cofmopolite, then, is a citizen of the world, or one who has banifhed from his breaft all partial private affections. One who loves his country, his family, his friends, and benefactors, only as they are parts of the whole, and can facrifice them without remorfe, whenever he conceives it will be promotive of the general good. The adoption of this nominal, but fictitious virtue, for fuch it is when oppofed to private duties, is an inftance of art not exceeded by any of the fu   Illuminifm. Its plaufibility renders it   ient mafk for men, deftitute of real goo   wifh to be thought poffeffed of the moft exalted virtue. It is a garment fuited to all the forms which thefe modern Proteufes can wifh to affume. It is a term replete with fallacy and deception, and is made to mean nothing, or any thing, as the illuminated poffeffor pleafes.

A principle of univerfal benevolence, or good will to being in general, doubtlefs enters into the compofition ; and, indeed, forms the foundation of all right focial affections. He who loves his friend merely from this confideration, that he is his friend, has no love to him as a fellow creature, and therefore, is deftitute of right focial affections.* But how is this principle of univerfal benevolence to be expreffed ? In the fame manner as the foldier

* A late European writer on this fubject obferves, that " Extended benevolence is the laft and moft perfect *fruit* of the private affections :" but if the tree be deftroyed the fruit certainly muft fail. And thus, according to this theory, if all private relations, and therewith private affections are deftroyed, extended, or univerfal benevolence cannot exift, unlefs there can be fruit without a tree, or an effect without a caufe. See Hall's Sermon on Infidelity, page 39.

My difapprobation of this fentiment, in which I have taken the liberty to diffent from this juftly celebrated writer, gives me an opportunity, which I gladly embrace, to recommend this moft excellent performance, as meriting at all times, and at the prefent in particular, the attention of mankind.

exprefles his attachment to the caufe in which
he is engaged, and to the army of which he is
a member; by firmly maintaining his poft,
and faithfully executing the orders of his com-
mander. To promote the general interefts of
mankind is to difcharge the duties of our re-
fpective ftations ; extending occafional aid, as
opportunity offers, to our fellow creatures in
diftrefs. On the contrary, he who neglects
the duties of his private fphere, ferves the public as the foldier does his caufe, who forfakes
his poft, and wanders through the ranks cre-
ating diforder and confufion.

Such is the modern Cofmopolite. Having
effectually eradicated all thofe narrow minded
prejudices which lead other men to be grate-
ful to their friends, to provide for their fami-
lies, and to ferve their country, his tafk of
focial duty is at an end, unlefs he fancies that
he is bound to labor for the general good, by
forming theories, projecting revolutions, or
removing the prejudices of mankind. The
things laft mentioned, become his duty, on
his fyftem, whenever he is pleafed to fancy
that they will be promotive of the general
good ; which juftifies the affertion, that Cofmopolitifm fignifies nothing, or any thing, as
the poffeffor pleafes.

The Cosmopolite, scorning the narrow
sphere of private duties which Providence has
appointed him, ascends the throne of the Supreme Ruler, and upon the great scale of universal being, judges for himself, what part belongs to him on the theatre of life.

On this ground we find Weishaupt justify-
ing his attempt to procure an abortion. He
confidently pleads, that what he did in that
affair, was no more than what he ought to
have done to secure his character, and seems
to claim no small degree of praise for doing
so much to preserve the order, of which he
was the founder, and which would have suffered extremely by his loss of reputation. The
same principle, in his view, would justify his
adepts, in plundering masonic funds, ecclesiastical revenues, and books and writings from
libraries. It was lawful, for the same reason,
to destroy the reputation of such as were opposed to his order, and to make use of pious
frauds to overcome men's prejudices against
the doctrines of Illuminism. Such practices,
which mankind have been accustomed to reprobate, were deeds of virtue in Weishaupt's
view, when done to promote the interests of
an institution calculated for the advancement
of human happiness.

France reasoned in the same manner. Having established this principle, that her revolution included whatever could exalt, refine, or bless mankind, in the fulness of her Cosmopolitism, she swore eternal enmity to kings; sent forth her emissaries to promote in other nations, insurrections against government; proffered protection and assistance to all promoters of revolutions, and even forced constitutions, framed in Paris, on those who neither desired, or would have received them but under the terrors of the bayonet. These benevolent plans have, indeed, been productive of the most cruel exactions, robberies, assassinations, violations of treaties, and indescribable scenes of misery; but it is a narrow minded prejudice, the French Philosopher will tell you, to compare these partial evils with the blessings of a revolution. This, gentle reader, is *Cosmopolitism.*

It is happy that these Cosmopolites cannot communicate their principles to the brutal race, lest they, leaving their proper charge to perish, should bestow their care where it is not needed. No; the great Author of nature, by indelible instinct, has taught them the same lesson of wisdom which he has addressed to our understandings, " *Let every one provide for*

his own houſe." It is happier ſtill that they
have not been able to tranſmit their univerſal
benevolence to other worlds, and to perſuade
the great luminary of our ſyſtem to wander
from his orbit, leaving us to froſt and darkneſs, to revolutionize other ſyſtems.   No ;
every creature, which has not rebelled againſt
the firſt great law of order, promotes the general good, by abiding in its preſcribed ſphere
of action.   Wherever this law is tranſgreſſed
ruin and miſery will be the conſequence.

This is the evidence on which we are to
form our judgment of the nature and tendency of Illuminiſm ; and what do we ſee, but a
deſtructive combination againſt the moſt precious intereſts of mankind ? It appears, that
the real nature and tendency of Illuminiſm is
to be found, by preciſely reverſing its oſtenſi-
ble aim, and the pretended object of its advocates.

By univerſal citizenſhip and diſintereſted
love, the Illuminee intends the deſtruction of
all whom he cannot render the dupes of his
deſigns. Morality, with him, means the unbounded indulgence of every corrupt bias of
human nature, only preſerving ſuch an exte-

rior as fhall better enable him to impofe on
mankind. The glorious emancipation from
flavery, to which he invites men, confifts in
the blind fubjection of all their actions to the
unknown fuperiors of the order. His humanity is the extinction of every tie of nature, of
every focial affection; even marriage is, in the
view of the Illuminee, an unfufferable monop-
oly, and every check to a brutal indulgence of
the fexual affections, a fpecies of tyranny.
His philofophy confifts of theories contradicted by univerfal experience. His religion is
atheifm dreffed to the tafte of the fcrupulous
confcience. His ufeful and important difcoveries, are new means of affaffination, abortion,
and peculation. His Creator is chance; and
his future glorious hope, everlafting fleep.

The original fource of Illuminifm, and the
principle which, in a greater or lefs degree,
influences all who are actuated by its genuine
fpirit, doubtlefs, is an innate enmity to Chriftianity, and a defire to be free from the checks
which its holy doctrines oppofe to the corruptions of the heart.

Motives different from this have, however,
united their operation in extending this com-

bination, efpecially in its hoftility to focial order, and an energetic government. Men who
wifh to poffefs property for which they have
not labored, and men of property who want
power, thefe, and men who never enjoy themfelves but in a ftorm, and whofe revolutionary
minds could not reft even in the calm of Para-
dife ; all of this defcription, find their feveral
ends promoted by difturbing the peace of fociety, removing the ancient land-marks, over-
turning ufeful eftablifhments, and breaking
down the barriers which have fecured the
rights and property of mankind.

For effecting thefe defigns, Illuminifm furnifhes a moft artful and fyftematic procefs. It
fupplies the want of power, by fubtle infinua-
tions. It teaches to bind men with invifible
bands ; to govern them by their prejudices
and paffions, and to delude them by a falfe
light, perpetually varying the object of purfuit, until the mind is loft in endlefs wander-
ings, and deprived of every permanent principle of action.

Another obfervable trait in the character of
thefe deceivers is, their pretended attachment
to the caufe they fecretly endeavor to under-

mine. Judging from their declarations, they appear the firm friends of government and religion, at the fame time that they are plying every fecret art to effect their deftruction. Thefe " pious frauds muft indeed be explained away," but this is eafily done among thofe to whom they have communicated the fpirit of the order.

C H A P. XII.

C H A P. XII.

OBJECTIONS CONSIDERED.

I AM fenfible that great efforts have been made, both in Europe and America, to convince mankind of the harmlefs nature of Illuminifm, and that its operation, whatever its tendency was, has long fince ceafed. But the wonderful zeal and bitternefs, which have been exhibited on this fubject, inftead of abating, juftly increafe fufpicion. If my neighbor fancies himfelf befet with ghofts and hobgoblins, I may well pity him, and endeavor to remove the painful illufion ; but is there any caufe for bitter refentment ? Shall I be at the pains of inventing, and circulating falfehoods to convince mankind that my neighbor's fears are imaginary ? That falfehoods of the groffeft nature have been moft induftrioufly propagated, and vengeance of the moft horrid kind denounced againft thofe who have exprefled their apprehenfions of the deftructive effects of Illuminifm, are facts. But why is it thus, if Illuminifm is that filly, harmlefs tale which by fome it is reprefented to be? Or why was not Robifon's work to be found in Germany? This is not the way to remove jealoufies. Where there is fuch a fluttering and outcry, we naturally conclude that fome are deeply wounded.

The peculiar invifibility of this order muft greatly invalidate the moft pofitive declarations in its favor, however honeftly intended. Admitting that Mr. Ebeling, in particular, is, as he afferts, neither an Illuminee nor a Mafon, and that his declarations on this fubject are the refult of conviction, muft this be admitted as conclufive evidence? A fimilar declaration has been made by many, in the uprightnefs of their hearts, who have been admitted even to the threfhold of the myfteries; for they have all along had the moft pofitive affurances, that the object of the order was the advancement of civil and religious liberty, in their moft perfect degrees.

Did thofe adepts, who retained their refpect for the fcriptures, believe that they were fupporting a fyftem of Spinozifm? or did initiated princes believe that they were protecting

P

an order which was aiming to reduce them to
the rank of plebeians? Yet persons of each of
the above descriptions gave their warm support to this Anti-Christian, disorganizing confederacy. Is then the judgment of professor
Ebeling to be deemed infallible?

From the peculiar nature of the subject, it
is obvious, that witnesses of the highest credibility in other matters, cannot be depended on
in this; here is so much collusion, art, and
studied concealment, that nothing but stub-
born facts, their own writings, and secret,
confidential communications, can be reasona-
bly admitted to be of weight in determining
the views of this order.

If Mr. Ebeling's proximity to the scene of
action, afforded him some special advantages
for estimating circumstantial evidence, is he
not likewise exposed, from this situation, to
some peculiar disadvantages? Doubtless he
had frequent, and most positive assurances
from many worthy and good men, men as
deserving the character, at least, as Weishaupt,
of whom he speaks so respectfully, that Illuminism was perfectly harmless, and even highly
beneficial to mankind. Is it not very possible
that such declarations, made with that subtle

fophiftry, and plaufibility in which Illuminifm
fo much abounds, fhould bias the judgment
of the charitable profeffor ? Then, in proportion to his nearnefs to the fuggefted, but un-
difcovered, danger, he would naturally become confident that it did not exift. It certainly adds importance to thefe obfervations,
that others, who had at leaft equal advantages
with Mr. Ebeling to judge of the real views of
thefe confpirators, yet differed much from
him in opinion.

But can thefe things be real ? Can human
nature be fo debafed, fo loft to every principle, not of religion only, but of focial virtue ?
Or could any perfon, capable of inventing
fuch a fyftem, imagine that it was practicable,
and that any confiderable number of mankind
would fubmit to fuch abominable impofitions ?
Thefe reflections, I confefs, are, to this moment, preffing on my mind, and raife a mo-
mentary doubt, which nothing but the moft
clear and indubitable evidence can remove.
But this doubt, we find upon reflection, arifes
more from the novelty of the fubject, than
from any thing in it that is really incredible. Is
not all wickednefs, madnefs and folly? Is not the
want of opportunity and abilities, the real caufe
why mankind do not exhibit more frequent
inftances of mifchievous madnefs ? Does the

hiftory of paft ages leave us room to wonder
at any act of extravagance, which is credibly
attefted, becaufe it is in the higheft degree un-
reafonable, and deftructive, both to the perpe-
trator and his fellow creatures? If revelation
has not fufficiently taught us *what is in man*,
the French revolution may furely convince us,
that there is no fpecies or degree of wickednefs, within the compafs of human ability,
which is beyond the corruption of the human
heart. Every impious, immoral, cruel, and
diforganizing fentiment, ever taught in the
fchool of Spartacus, has been exemplified in
late tranfactions which have taken place in
Europe.

It is not, indeed, to be fuppofed that all the
proceedings of the fociety were minutely conformable to the adopted fyftem : we know
they were not. The machine was too un-
wieldy to be applied in all cafes. The heads
of the order referved a right of deviating
according to their judgment of circumftances.
Some needed not Weifhaupt's procefs of
feduction, to prepare them for the higheft myfteries of Illuminifm. A complete fyftem may
be ufeful as a general directory, even when it
is not brought into univerfal operation. In
this inftance the vanity of the author, doubtlefs
excited him to render his work perfect, and

connected in all its parts. The objection
which fome make to the exiftence of Illuminifm, that it is too complicated and cumber-
fome ever to attain the object afcribed to the
projector, cannot be important.

While the Illuminees complain of great
feverity in the proceedings of the government
againft their order, others, judging of the
degree of the crime by the punifhment, conclude, from the lightnefs of the latter, that the
former could not be equal to what has been
reprefented. Deprivation of office, imprifon-
ment, and fome inftances of banifhment,
appear indeed to have been punifhments inadequate to fuch attrocious confpiracies. Weifhaupt himfelf expected nothing fhort of the
gallows in cafe of his detection. That his
expectations were not realized, was, doubtlefs,
owing in part, to the fecret influence of Illuminifm over the meafures of government; and
ftill more, to the many refpectable characters
found to be partially involved, which rendered it expedient that the fubject fhould be
treated with all poffible lenity.

In addition to this, it is to be obferved, that
the weaknefs and inferiority of many of the
German principalities, reduce them to the

P 2

neceffity of accommodating the meafures of
government to particular circumftances. On
the authority of private letters from Germany,
Barruel relates, That the Duke of Brunfwick,
in particular, juftified his not proceeding to
extremities with the Illuminees in his ftates,
by faying, " Suppofing I fhould fend them
away, they would only go elfewhere and calum-
niate me ;" adding, " a league ought to be entered into by the German princes, to fuffer
them in no part of the Empire."*

* Barruel's Memoirs, Vol. IV. p. 317.

C H A P. XIII.

Collateral Proofs, and General Observations, in rela-
tion to Europe.

THE evidence, and authentic documents,
which have been exhibited, it is conceived are
fuch, as can leave no doubt of the exiftence
and active operation of Illuminifm from 1776,
until thefe works of darknefs were brought
to light, and their promoters compelled to
change their mode of procedure. Moft of the
late European writers, where propriety would
permit, allude to it as an indubitable fact. It
is not, indeed, denied even by thofe who feem
moft difpofed to quiet our apprehenfions on this
fubject: their efforts are directed to prove,
either that its operation is now at an end, or,
that it never was defigned to produce, nor
was indeed capable of producing, the evils
afcribed to it. Whether the fubverfion of
fuperftition and defpotifm was the whole aim
of thefe plotting geniufes, their writings and
conduct will enable us to judge.

The statements and observations in this chapter are principally designed to shew, that the contagious poison is still spreading and infecting society, threatening the destruction of every thing important to mankind, and therefore, that the history of this sect is a subject highly interesting.

Admitting that the order of the Illuminees is now extinct, their systems and doctrines remain; the books by which they communicated their poison are in circulation; the arts by which they inveigled and corrupted the minds of men are not forgotten, and the former members of this society still possess the skill, the wicked subtlety, to which the care of Weishaupt formed his adepts. To prove that such destructive arts have existed, is virtually to prove that they still exist; that is, that the care and caution of the wise and good ought to be the same, as if they were assured of their present existence and actual operation. Can it be a doubt whether wicked men will use the most effectual weapons in their power? Whether they will adopt those means which they judge best calculated to promote their purposes? It belongs to the art of fortification to provide against every possible mode of attack. The invention of artillery

pointed out the necessity of new means of defence, and it became the engineer to conftruct
works, which would repel their deftructive
violence. The legiflator, the inftructor of
youth, the moralift, the defender of chriftianity, have new arts to encounter, new modes
of attack and inftruments of mifchief to guard·
againft; how neceffary, then, that they fhould
become acquainted with the weapons of their
enemies, and of their new modes of attack?

Although the diffolution of this combination has been confidently afferted, the evidence
of the fact does not appear. The interruption
it has received from detection, would naturally produce an increafe of caution; but can it
be fuppofed to effect any change in the wifhes
or defigns of the confpirators? Is the thing in
itfelf probable? The proof adduced is merely
of the negative kind, and much of this is contradicted by plain facts.

In 1794, it was announced to the public, that
from 1790, "every concern of the Illuminees
had ceafed." But in addition to what has
been already related of a contrary afpect,
many circumftances contradict this affertion.

In 1791, a ſpark of Illuminiſm caught in
Ireland, and ſpread with aſtoniſhing rapidity,
threatening a univerſal conflagration. The
conſpirators there aſſumed the denomination
of United Iriſhmen.* This extenſive combination was concealed under forms very ſimilar to thoſe of Maſonry, and the whole was
methodized upon the graduated ſcale of Illuminiſm.

The ſubordinate ſocieties conſiſted of thirty
members, and were under the direction of a
Baronial committee, compoſed of a delegate

* See the report of the Committee of Secrecy, preſented to the Iriſh Houſe of Commons, July, 1797, with the
papers and teſtimonies upon which ſaid report was founded : 2d. edit. London, 1798, for John Stockdale ; and the
Speech of the Lord Chancellor, Feb. 19, 1798, reprinted
for J. Stockdale.

What is here introduced in relation to Ireland, is not
deſigned to intimate that the people of that country did
not need a redreſs of grievances. It is noticed merely as
an evidence of the exiſtence of Illuminiſm. It originated
from foreign influence. The ſyſtem adopted was perfectly in the ſtyle of the new order. The paſſions of the people were inflamed, and their judgments blinded by miſ-
repreſentations. They were deceived as to the real object
of their leaders. By the ſame means inſurrections may be
excited under any government where the people are in
a ſimilar ſtate of vice and ignorance.

from each fociety within the Barony. The Baronial committees in each county, in like manner elected delegates, who formed a county committee. Delegates from each county committee, formed, in like manner, a provincial committee for the government and direction of the feveral county committees, in each of the four provinces ; and thefe provincial directories appointed the general executive, whofe refidence was in the metropolis.

The fecretaries of each of thefe committees, were to be taken from an higher committee, and by them the whole correfpondence was maintained, and the orders of the executive tranfmitted through the different degrees. Thefe orders, for the greater fecurity, were, if poffible, to be communicated verbally, or otherwife, to be immediately deftroyed.

One object of the union fpecified in the conftitution was, that of communicating with fimilar focieties in other parts, and particularly with the Jacobin club at Paris. In addition to the ufual oaths of fecrecy, fubmiffion, &c. every member was folemnly fworn never to give evidence againft a brother, in any court of juftice, *whatever might be his crime.*

Another requisite oath was *fidelity to the French republic.**

In April, 1796, the outline of a treaty with France was drawn up by the general committee of the union, and tranfmitted to the French directory, in confequence of which a French force made its appearance at Bantry Bay, on the 24th of December, but by a miftake between the parties, with refpect to the time agreed upon for the invafion, the Infurgents were not prepared to co-operate, and the expedition failed. The accounts detailed in the reports of the feveral committees, reprefent the numbers of this affociation to be vaftly numerous. It is particularly ftated, that 150,000 were organized and enrolled in the province of Ulfter.†

Similar focieties, in clofe union and correfpondence with this, were formed in England, and Scotland, under different names, but purfuing the fame object. ·

A ftatement, ftill more interefting to Americans, is found in the report of a provincial

* Chancellor's Speech, p. 32—Irifh report, Appendix, No. 4.

† Appendix, No. 31.

meeting, dated Randolftown, August 14, 1797, from which it appears, that a number of focieties were formed in *North America*, from which, in the laft eight days, *two hundred and eleven dollars* had been received.*

The oftenfible object of this union, was a parliamentary reform ; but the correfpondence with the directory, and the teftimony of feveral witneffes, afford abundant proof, that this was held up merely to blind the people, and that the real object of the *chiefs* was, a revolution, of which the French revolution was to be the model.

Barruel relates feveral inftances in which the adepts were found fomenting confpiracies againft the government, both in Auftria and Pruffia, long after the ceffation of all the operations of Illuminifm were announced to the public. Thefe attempts were truly formidable, and were rendered abortive, only by thofe ftrange accidental occurrences, by which a governing Providence difappoints the devices of the crafty. One inftance is worthy of notice, as a curiofity. Mehalovich, formerly

Q

* Appendix, No. 14.

a capuchin, was a principal in a conspiracy
in Germany. While he was out one day, a
domestic, playing with one of his fellow ser-
vants, for the sake of humor, put on the
capuchin habit, which his master had preserved among his clothes, when his master unex-
pectedly returned. The servant, in order to
prevent being discovered with the habit, hid
himself under the bed. Mehalovich, with
two other conspirators, entered the room ;
and thinking themselves secure, they con-
versed, unreservedly, upon the conspiracy,
which was to break out in three days. Mehalovich took five hundred thousand florins,
which were hidden in a harpsichord, and gave
them to one of the conspirators for the execution of the plan. After they left the room,
the servant went immediately and discovered
the whole plot to the ministers of state. In
the result, Mehalovich, with eight accompli-
ces, was executed, and many others were
condemned to exile, or to perpetual imprit-
onment.

This conspiracy exhibits a remarkable instance of the means by which modern revolutions have been effected. The party, desirous
of a new order of things, through their influence at court, found means of forming a
garrison in Vienna, of substantial and honest

citizens, little accuftomed to bear arms. Thefe
new raifed corps, they treated with the greateft
feverity, under the pretence, that what they
did was by the order of the emperor ; hoping
by this to render the government obnoxious
to them.*

Habitually viewing Europeans as deprived
of the rights of men, and groaning under
oppreffion, our attention has been naturally
diverted from confidering the real character of
modern revolutionifts, and the tendency of
their meafures and principles. From the happy fuccefs of their own revolution, Americans, in particular, have incautioufly indulged
the idea, that a revolution muft meliorate fociety ; that nothing more is neceffary to render men free, profperous, and happy, than to
overturn ancient eftablifhments. Even under
the adminiftrations of WASHINGTON and AD-
AMS, thefe children of change, fancied a revolution neceffary to preferve our liberties.
But what has been exhibited in Europe, may
teach us that it is time to paufe, and confider
confequences.

Would the deluded people of Ireland probably have improved their fituation by overturn-

* Barruel's Memoirs, Vol. IV. p. 311, 312.

ing their own government, and throwing themselves into the arms of France? What recompence has France herself found for her slaugh-
tered millions, her exhausted treasuries, and
the scenes of indescribable distress which have
attended her revolution? Can a people enjoy,
or preserve the blessings of temperate liberty,
until they are enlightened and virtuous? Will
unprincipled, ambitious men exert the influence they gain over mankind, to make them
free or happy? Have none but tyrants reafon to dread this new, revolutionizing
spirit? Was not Switzerland free? Were the
magistrates of Geneva despots? In fine, is
that revolutionary power, which consists in
blinding its agents, and inflaming the bad
passions of a nation by false representations,
desirable in any government?

If opposition to constituted authorities, and
a pretended zeal for the rights of men, are
proofs of patriotism and benevolence, the
present may well be called *the golden age;* but
we have been sufficiently entertained with
vague declamations, it is time to attend to facts
and experience.

It is obvious that society cannot subsist, unless those are governed who will not govern
themselves. Were all the members of a com-

munity invariably difpofed to practice right-
coufnefs, to fuch a community, a government
of reftraint would be unneceffary. On the
contrary, a fociety compofed of men of an
oppofite character, need the ftrong hand of
power to preferve the public tranquillity.
Such a government tends indeed to abufe,
and perhaps there may not be an inftance,
where this rigorous exercife of authority is
maintained, with a perfect regard to juftice
and the rights of the fubject. It is to be
regretted that men, invefted with power, are
fo little difpofed to approve themfelves the
fathers and benefactors of their fubjects. But
is it therefore defirable, in the prefent ftate
of mankind, that every government fhould
be revolutionized into a republic ? Is the modern, fafhionable oath, of " hatred to all kings,"
dictated by an enlightened and chriftian benevolence? That man might as reafonably lay claim
to benevolence, who fhould loofe the hands of
a mad-man, and fet him at liberty to deftroy his
family and himfelf. Until a people are enlightened and virtuous, republican freedom will
degenerate into licentioufnefs, and afford an
opportunity to the factious and ambitious,
by enflaming the paffions of men, to erect a
tyranny more to be dreaded than that of the
moft arbitrary defpot on earth.

Q 2

No nation in modern Europe has suffered more from an unlimited monarchy than France ; but, separate from all the mischiefs which her mad politics have produced to other parts of the world, there certainly has been no equal period under her most despotic kings, productive of evils, to be compared with those which have attended the late revolution ; and these evils must probably have continued, if general BONAPARTE had not fortunately acquired such unlimited control over the nation, as has restored order and peace.

It is futile to attempt to avoid the conclusion, which this fact affords, by observing, that these evils are to be imputed, not to the people of France, but to factious leaders, who have made them the dupes of their ambitious views ; for it is the wretched ignorance, and depravity of a people which make them dupes of such leaders. How gross must be the ignorance of a people who can believe, that such men as Danton, Marat, and Robespierre, are friends to real liberty, and the rights of man ? A vitiated society will always have such leaders. We may safely estimate the character of a people, by that of the persons in whom they place confidence. This con-

fideration alone, proves, that virtue and in‑
formation are neceſſary to the fupport of a
free government. Where thefe are want‑
ing, perfons of the above defcription will
never fail, by the cry of tyranny, and a
pretended zeal for equal rights, to increafe
the jealoufy of a people againſt rulers of their
own choice ; to withdraw from them the
neceſſary confidence, and to transfer that confi‑
dence, moſt improperly indeed, to themfelves,
To this evil, republican governments, from
the lenity and indulgence which enters into
their conſtitution, have always been peculiarly
expofed ; but the danger is greatly augmented
fince the arts of deception have been wrought
into a fyſtem, and the active *Propaganda* of
Illuminifm has been laboring to undermine
every government within the reach of its in‑
fluence. From this caufe, every confiderable
republic in Europe has undergone a revolu‑
tion ; and the prefervation of governments of
a more rigorous form, is owing to their greater
energy in repelling the invading enemy.

The American revolution took place under
the happieſt omens. It did not originate from
the blinding influence of defigning men ; it
was not excited by the ambitious defire of
rendering America miſtrefs of the world ;

but it owed its riſe and progreſs to a juſt
ſenſe, in the Americans, of the rights of men,
of what was due to themſelves, and to poſter-
ity, and a wiſe, patriotic, and virtuous determination to reſiſt the firſt encroachments of
arbitrary power. Simplicity of manners,
habits of economy, induſtry, and moderation,
together with ample means of information,
of moral and religious inſtruction, every circumſtance ſeemed to promiſe permanency to
our government, and a rich harveſt of the
bleſſings of freedom. Never was the experiment of a republican government made with
fairer proſpects of ſucceſs. Yet, even here
has anarchy reared her horrid front, and
ſtruck terror into the hearts of Americans.
The arts of intrigue have withdrawn public
confidence from approved worth, and tried
merit, and all the energies of government
have been called into action to ſuppreſs a ſpirit
of inſurrection, and open oppoſition to con-
ſtitutional meaſures.

There yet appears a large number of citizens, we hope a great majority, who ſeem
ſenſible of the importance of electing men of
principle, and of ſupporting the moral, and religious inſtitutions of our country : and while
ſuch is our ſituation, we are not to deſpair of
the republic.

It is far from the defign of thefe obfervations, to prove, that a republican government is either undefirable, or impracti-
cable; they are intended merely to exhibit the
abfurdity of the idea, which many have adopted, that nothing more is neceffary to make
any people happy than to reject their own
government, and receive a conftitution from
France. Whatever may be the refult of the
experiment now making in America, the
events which have taken place here, as well as
in Europe, give weight to the opinion, that
mankind are not generally prepared for the
enjoyment of republican bleffings.

But it is not merely by exciting revolutions
and confpiracies, that Illuminifm has difcovered itfelf in Europe, fince we were told, " that
all the concerns of the Illuminees had ceafed."

So late as February, 1798, the magiftrates
of Jena were compelled to punifh a number of
the ftudents of that univerfity, who had formed an affociation, by the name of Amicifts,
under the direction of fome Illuminee. They
had been taught to confider the oath of their
affociation as fuperceding all others, even the
moft facred engagement that could be made.
The form of this fociety was mafonic; and by

their secretary, they maintained a regular correspondence with other lodges. Their code
taught them to confider themfelves as a ftate
within a ftate ; enjoined the moft profound
fecrecy, and exprefsly required, that, fhould
feveral of them afterwards refide in the fame
town, they fhould eftablifh a lodge, and do all
in their power to propagate the fociety.*

On the authority of fome private communications from Germany, the hiftorian further
ftates, that the univerfity at Halle, was in a
fimilar fituation with that at Jena. That public infults were offered by the ftudents, to the
minifters of religion, while attending the duties of their office ; that dogs were fet at
them while preaching, and that indecencies,
took place in the churches, which would not
be fuffered in the ftreets.†

The very refpectable writer before quoted,
of Upper Saxony, fays, " In the great univerfities of Germany, which I have feen, or of
which I have had any information, the ftu-

* See Minutes of the Judgment of Hamburg, No. 45.
March 13.

† Barruel's Memoirs, Vol. IV. p. 306—316.

dents have the appearance of a set of rude and
insolent Jacobins. In some universities, where
the students amount to about a thousand or
twelve hundred, they are all formed into private societies ; and that, in all the German
universities, the chief study is the new system
of philosophy, by which the mind is totally
bewildered, and at length deprived of every
solid principle of religion, morality, or sound
politics. Unfortunately," he adds, "the clergy,
and many, even of those who serve the country parishes, have had their minds bewildered
with the metaphysical jargon of the universities. They have come to doubt, and some to
deny, the truths of Christianity itself ; and to
assert, that it is a vulgar superstition, adapted
only to the ignorant. The Old Testament has
very generally lost its authority ; and a country clergyman, lately in company with a
friend of mine, laughed heartily at the ignorance and confined notions of the clergy of
the church of England, when he heard they
still believe the Mosaic history of the fall
of man."*

A gentleman of great respectability in Europe, in a letter to his correspondent in A-

* Appendix to Anti-Jacobin Review, Vol. VI. p. 569.

merica, dated September, 1800, says, " I lament
exceedingly, the too plain state of the public
mind on the great points of religion and morality. Religion has been so freely dealt with
now in Germany, that it no longer makes the
impreffion of former times, always mixed
with fome tincture of veneration. It is now
entered upon with the fame coolnefs and eafe
as any other matter of fcientific difcuffion.
This of itfelf is a misfortune. It was furely
of advantage to us, that the mind could not
engage in any religious refearch, without fome-
what of the fame referve (call it fuperftition if
you will) that one feels when difcuffing a
point of filial duty or relation. Religion
having thus loft all its ufe, it has even ceafed
to occupy its former fhare of room in the
German Catalogues ; and the fcribblers have
fairly begun to treat the plain *moral* duties
with the fame freedom. I received lately, a
a fmall performance, by one Emmering, at
Franckfort, who, even under the tyranny of
Cuftine, in 1792, had the boldnefs to attack
the profligate fpeeches of Bohmer and Forfter,
in the Convention of Mentz. He ftill pre-
ferves the fame unfubdued fpirit ; and though
a layman, (a Wine merchant) he nobly main-
tains the caufe of religion and virtue. In this
little performance he mentions feveral moft

profligate publications, in which the fidelity of
the husband, to the marriage bed, is fyftemat-
ically fhewn to be a frivolous prudery ; and
therefore, concubinage, or polygamy, perfectly
proper, under certain regulations, purely civil ;
and, which is moft lamentable, the proper courts,
before which this was brought by Emmering
himfelf, refufed to take it up as a public offence. This, at Franckfort, grieved me ; for,
during the revolution at Mentz, the inhabitants of Franckfort, behaved in a manner that
is not exceeded by any thing on record."

" I was the more affected by this, becaufe I
found that Knigge and Weifhaupt, after having formed very high expectations from their
operations in Edeffa, were difappointed ; and,
in 1782, reprobate Edeffa in the moft rancorous terms. Philo fays, " the inhabitants are
too rich, too republican, and will not be led
about by the nofe."

" Emmering mentions another publication
by one Semler, proveffedly written to weaken
the parental tie, laying it down as a principle, that a man's children have only an artifi-
cial title to his fortune, unlefs they have aided
him in the acquifition of it. But the ftate, by
giving that protection by which the fruits of

R

his industry are secured to him, has a preferable and natural claim. The aim of this unnatural principle is too barefaced, I think, to be dangerous. But a companion to it by George Forster, is most atrocious. The sons and daughters are made the judges of their parent's character and conduct, and if they find either *incivic*, they are peculiarly bound to denounce them as undutiful to them (their children) by giving them pernicious principles and education. I mention these things to shew how the profligate monsters have attempted to revolutionize *the mind of man.*"

We have many unequivocal proofs that this is a just representation of the state of religion and literature in Germany. To what views and motives shall we then attribute the conduct of those gentlemen, who endeavor to compel us, by illiberal reproaches, to believe their unsupported declarations ? Do they not know that the mind naturally revolts against such unreasonable violence, such tyrannical attempts to hoodwink our understandings ?

C H A P. XIV.

Collateral Proofs, and General Obfervations, relating to the United States.

THOSE who affure us that Illuminifm was always harmlefs, and has long fince been extinct in Europe, at the fame time ridicule the idea of its having ever exifted in America, or had any influence on our civil or religious interefts. From the peculiar fecrecy of the fect, thefe gentlemen came forward with the greateft advantages for gaining credit ; for, they confidently afk, where are thefe Illumi-nees ? Point them out to us. With the fame confidence they affert that we were ignorant of the name of this order until it was communicated by Robifon. This is true, but if they are impartial, Why do they not lay open the whole truth ? Why do they not tell us that the ftrength of the order lies principally in concealment, and that it affumes any name or form, rather than its own proper one ? Why do they not tell us, what they very well know, that, even in their native foil, Bavaria, their name and exiftence were equally un-known, till their deeds difcovered their retreat, and induced an inquiry, which brought to light their hidden works of darknefs ? The inquiry before us does not refpect names and appellations. We are not contending that there are, or have been, men in America, known as Illuminees. The important fact is, that men in America, under the direction and influence of a foreign head, are, or at leaft have been, combined in oppofition to our peace, profperity and welfare. A rafh, un-founded fuggeftion of this nature would be highly criminal ; it is here made with folem-nity, and under a conviction, that the evidence by which it is fupported, affords juft caufe of alarm.

Upon the lift of illuminated lodges, furnifh-ed by Dr. Robifon, feveral are mentioned as exifting in America before 1786.*

The zeal with which Dr. Morfe has invefti-gated this matter, as it refpects this country, though it has loaded him with that kind of obloquy which is the good man's praife, has

* Robifon's Proofs. p. 159.

furnifhed fome important documents with which we fhall enrich this part of the fubject.

In an Appendix to his Faft Sermon, of May 9, 1798, he gives us a particular account of the lodge WISDOM, inftituted at Portfmouth in Virginia, as early as 1786, a branch of the Grand Orient of France, and numbered the 2660th defcendant of that ftock.* From an original letter, for the authenticity of which he pledges himfelf to the public, he has furnifhed us with an official lift of the numbers, names, ages, places of nativity, and profeffions of the officers and members of this lodge, together with their horrid feal, in which, with fome of the ufual mafonic fymbols, are interwoven emblems of carnage and death. The members of this lodge, confifting of one hundred, were chiefly emigrants from France and St. Domingo. This lodge had a deputy refiding with the mother fociety in France, to communicate all needful inftructions. Two fimilar focieties had originated from the Portfmouth lodge, one in Virginia, the other at St. Domingo,

R 2

* Particular mention is made of this lodge by Barruel, Vol. IV. p. 213.

By the fame means he had evidence of the
exiftence of a fimilar fociety at New York,
called " The Grand Orient of New York,"
derived, in like manner, from the lodge of the
fame name in France. From this New York
lodge iffued a French lodge, called the UNION,
which was the 14th branch from this feconda-
ry ftock. The particular location of the other
lodges, or whether the number here fpecified,
included the whole which were then in America, were not known.

It is an important item of information,
which the Doctor further communicates on
this fubject, that the beft informed Free Mafons among us, difclaim thefe focieties; the
titles of fome of their dignitaries, their feal
and motto they declare are not mafonic. In
the clofe he introduces the following calculation, which, though obvious, is interefting.
Admitting all thefe American lodges, individ-
ually, to contain an equal number of members
with the lodge Wifdom, the calculation gives
at that time, no lefs than 1700 agents of Illuminifm in America, in clofe connection and
correfpondence with each other, and with the
Grand Orient at Paris, from which they received conftant *illumination*; and we may

add, acting under the influence of a fociety, which was the active foul and vital fpring of thofe fcenes of horror exhibited in France and other parts of Europe.

A very refpectable Mafon, formerly Grand Mafter of all the lodges in the State in which he refided, informed me, that a letter, defigned for one of the abovementioned lodges, fell into his hands while he was Grand Mafter, by a very natural miftake, and which left him no room to doubt the accuracy and authenticity of what Dr. Morfe has ftated on this fubject. He could not afcertain particulars, as the time of his receiving the letter was previous to the difcovery of Illuminifm, and confequently it appeared more enigmatical than it probably would at prefent ; and fince that time, it has been miflaid, or taken out of his pofleffion.

The following facts, received from unqueftionable authority, confirm the truth and accuracy of the above reprefentation.   A gentleman of high refpectability, who fays, " he belonged to a lodge of the *ancient* order of Mafons," and was in a fituation to know perfectly the character and conduct of the Portfmouth lodge, under date of March 23, 1800, writes thus to Dr. Morfe ; " The lodge in

Portfmouth, to which you allude, in your appendix, called the French lodge, was confidered by me as under the *modern term of majonry.* Its members, in 1789, were moftly French. Some men who were refpectable, and attached to our government, Dickfon and Cox, particularly, belonged to the lodge at that time. It is probable about the time Admiral Cambis' fleet arrived there from St. Domingo, there might have been many enthufiaftic Frenchmen admitted, which fwell the number in your lift."

April 11, 1800, the fame gentleman writes, " That you had good grounds to fufpect the defigns of the French lodge at Portfmouth in Virginia, I have no reafons, nor ever had, to doubt; and, at a time, it is evident to me, that their work was to effect the plans of France in this country; and that the bulk of the members who compofed the lodge in 1797, were ready to further any defigns which the French government may have had on this country, and to give their aid to carry them into effect, as they were moftly Frenchmen. The few Americans admitted were *to prevent their being fufpected,* and they could operate without them; as I am convinced they never were admitted to the higheft degrees."

Add to the above, that this French lodge at Portsmouth, was not in fellowship with the other lodges of the *ancient* order of Masons; and that one of its members from Germany, at a period when Americans generally thought favorably of the French revolution, declared, (and the declaration can be substantiated) that he belonged to a lodge in Germany, in which that revolution was planned. These facts, and those originally stated, together with credible information, received direct from the most respectable men in Portsmouth, prove incontestibly the correctness of the account which has been published of this lodge.

Although the above documents have never been confronted with any evidence, unless clamor and abuse may be so called, yet, as this mode of reasoning has its influence with some people, I must beg leave to introduce another respectable masonic testimony. It is an extract, furnished by a friend, from a printed oration, delivered February 3d, A. L. 5801, before the Grand Royal Arch Chapter for the state of New-York, by the Rev. John F. Ernst, Grand Chaplin. The friend who furnishes the extract, writes, that he (the orator) " is held in high, very high estima-

tion by the Mafons in thofe parts." The
orator, guarding his brethren againft the
wrong ufe which he acknowledges has been
made of Mafonry, in many inftances, introduces the following fentence.

"The unravelled and deep defigns of *modern*
Mafons, called the Illuminati, who have almoft
inundated Europe, *and are gaining ground faft
in America,* have clearly demonftrated the
abufe, *untyled Mafon lodges have met with;* and
how they, when not prefided over, and
guarded by men of knowledge, and genuine
mafonic principles, *can* be overthrown, revolutionized, and *moulded according to pleafure.*"

Are thefe documents deferving no credit?
Shall we renounce our reafon, becaufe fome
men will not believe unlefs they have a
fign from heaven? And if true, do they not
afford juft caufe of alarm? Admitting this
was a full difcovery of the extent of Illuminifm in America, at that time, and that fince
that time, it has received no increafe, which
is far from being probable; is a body of
feventeen hundred men, acting with the force
of fecret focieties, and under the direction of
a foreign power, compatible with the peace,
quiet, and fafety of this country? We need

no longer wonder at the confidence the French Directory expreffed in their *diplomatic fkill* and influence in America, or the prevalence of the new philofophy, and the alarming change which has taken place here, in the ftate of religion and morals. It is no longer furprifing, that every method has been adopted to excite oppofition to the meafures of the late adminiftration of our government, to vilify our beft characters, and to alienate the minds of the citizens from their rulers; or, that native Americans have been compelled to yield their feats to foreigners. This affords an eafy explanation, of what, without this key, muft appear myfterious, that a period, in which we have enjoyed all that men can enjoy of the blefings of a free and excellent government, attended with a degree of profperity, which has fcarce its parallel in the hiftory of mankind, has been a period of complaint, of tumult and infurrection. Nor is it unaccountable that we fhould hear it afferted, with the higheft effrontery, that our greateft danger arifes, not from France, from Illuminifm, or felf-created focieties, but, from the tyranny of the clergy, and from Britifh influence. Thefe are among the known arts of Illuminifm. Whoever has carefully ob-ferved its progrefs in Europe, will eafily

difcern the features of the monfter, under all
its concealments. It is an axiom in Illuminifm, upon which its difciples, both in Europe and America, have formed their practice, that the moft egregious and abfurd
falfehoods, if told with confidence, and confidently repeated, will at length gain credit
and influence.

As has been ftated, we have ample proof,
that focieties have exifted in America, derived
from the Grand Orient in France, and inti-
mately connected with that directing head of
all the improved, or illuminated lodges in
France. This evidence, coming from different
quarters and diftinct fources, is greatly cor-
roberated by that circumftance, and acquires
an additional claim to our belief. But will
it be faid, becaufe illuminated focieties, connected with thofe in France, once exifted in
America, it is not therefore certain that they
were united in defign with the parent
fociety, or wifhed to extend the empire of
Illuminifm ? Though Jacobin clubs were
fuddenly formed in every part of the United
States, fimilar to thofe in France, by means
of which, the Jacobins governed the nation at
their pleafure, yet this, it may with as much
truth be faid, is no demonftration that the

clubs in America were formed for the like purpofe. Thus men reafon, who are determined not to admit conviction. But can any perfon, not blinded by prejudice, doubt whence arofe the oppofition made to the adoption of the federal conftitution, and to every meafure, calculated to eftablifh the independence, profperity, and refpectability of our country? It is not commonly to be expected, that we fhould be able to fubftantiate, by legal evidence, the fecret machinations of the emiffaries of darknefs. Their intentions are not to be difcovered by their profeffions, and oftenfible character; but often they unwarily expofe themfelves to the wakeful eye of wifdom.

Before the fyftematical arrangements of Illuminifm became public, the active interference of France in America was vifible to every perfon of difcernment, who was not oppofed to conviction. It is well known that the activity of Genet, by granting commiffions to privateers, procuring the enlifment of foldiers, forming clubs, extending the influence of France, and by his attempts to excite oppofition to government, and to alienate the minds of the people from their rulers, produced a remonftrance on the fubject

s

from our watchful Prefident, which rendered
his recal unavoidable. To exculpate thofe
under whofe commiffion Genet acted, his
conduct in America has been attributed to his
imprudently exceeding his commiffion. This
is eafily faid, as many other things have been,
without a coloring of truth. Genet had his
recommendation for the American appointment, in the proofs he had given of his diforganizing qualities at Geneva, where he had
been the fuccefsful agent of the fame deteftable
policy. But we are not left to conjectures
refpecting the grounds of his appointment.
Robefpierre, wifhing to crufh the Briffotine
faction, that he might poffefs their power and
influence, charges them with their unjuft
attempts againft other governments, and with
refpect to America, fays exprefsly, " Genet,
their agent at Philadelphia, made himfelf chief
of a club there, and never ceafed to make and
excite motions equally injurious and perplex-
ing to the government."

Defeated in this attempt, by the vigilance
of WASHINGTON, but not difcouraged, rendered more cautious, but not lefs malicious,
the agents of France ftill purfued, though
with greater fecrecy, their diforganizing
fyftem. In 1795, Fauchet's intercepted letter

again difclofed their dark defigns, and the
real character of " the pretended patriots of
America." The memorable fentence, relating
to the infurgents in the weftern counties, will
not be foon forgotten. He informs his government, that the weftern people, " Republicans by principle, independent by character
and fituation, they could not but accede with
enthufiafm to the criminations which we
have fketched."* The grievances of thefe
deluded people, or their criminations of government, were not, it appears, fuggefted by
their own feelings, but by *French agents*, who
dictated to them what were the cenfurable
proceedings of their conftituted authorities.

This is not the firft time this officious
nation has fketched grievances, and excited
thofe who were at reft, to arm themfelves
againft their own governments. But left this
fketch fhould not meet the feelings, and obtain
the full approbation of thefe republicans,
Fauchet adminifters to his employers, this
further confolation, that " thefe complaints
were fyftematizing by the converfation of
influential men, who retired into thofe wild
countries, and who, from principle, or by a
feries of particular heart-burnings, animated dif-
contents, already too near to effervefcence."†

* Fauchet's Letter, 19th parag.   † ibid. 12th parag.

It muft now be left with the reader to determine, whether or not he will allow Mr.
Fauchet, and his influential coadjutors, the
praife he claims of exciting an infurrection,
which coft the United States more than a
million of dollars.

As Mr. Fauchet has not told us what arguments his influential agents would ufe to
promote the infurrection, the defect may be
fupplied by the following communication,
made by a gentleman of accurate information,
and of the firft refpectability in Pennfylvania;
who warrants us to affure the public, that
" *the plunder of the city of Philadelphia was prom-
ifed to the Infurgents in 1794, by their leaders.*"

The focieties of United Irifhmen next mark
the progrefs of Illuminifm in America. In
May, 1798, the declaration and conftitution
of the American Society of United Irifhmen
were difcovered, and publifhed in Philadelphia.
This fociety was evidently founded on the
principles of the Illuminated lodges in Europe;
and we are not left in the dark as to their
object; for no one, who will attentively read
their conftitution, can hefitate to fay, it was
to enlift and organize the difcontented and
factious, and particularly *foreigners*, in the

different parts of the United States, in order to diffufe the fpirit, and promote the infernal defigns, of Illuminifm in this country. Their conftitution is drawn up with confiderable ingenuity. The oftenfible object of their affociation, was to act in concert with their United brethren in Ireland. "*Equality* and *Liberty* to ALL men," was, at the fame time, held forth in their declaration; and in their *teft*, each member pledged himfelf, that he would direct all his efforts to the "attainment of *liberty* and *equality to* MANKIND, *in whatever country he may refide.*" The fection which immediately follows the *teft*, exhibits a ftrong evidence, that the *oftenfible* object of the fociety, was not the *real* one; and, that under the femblance of humanity, was concealed a project far from the emancipation of mankind. The fection is this: "That the *teft* of this fociety, and the *intention* of this *inftitution*, (in all other refpects than as a *focial body*, attached to freedom) be confidered as *fecret* and *inviolable*, in all cafes, but between members, and in the body of the fociety." The exiftence of this fociety, the intended fecrecy of its defigns, and the evident tendency of its labors, exhibit further, and ftrong proof, that the baneful influence of *Illuminifm* is diffufing itfelf through this country.

Although our ears were daily wounded with the difgufting extravagancies of France, and our property fubjected to the moft wanton fpoilations, ftill, from fome fecret caufe, her influence was prevailing in America ; when the directory, mifled by the fhameful pliancy of our ambaffador,* entirely mifcalculated their influence, and the remaining energy of the American character. Sure of their prey, they too foon threw off the mafk which concealed their defigns. Their conduct towards the American Envoys, who were fent to demand a redrefs of grievances, was fo repugnant to every fentiment of juftice, good faith and propriety, as to admit of no apology. The mift, which had been gathering around the minds of Americans, and through which France appeared great and magnanimous, was diffolved in a moment. In vain was recourfe had to the deceptive arts which heretofore had been fo fuccefsful. Her deteftable policy filenced her advocates, and united all who regarded righteoufnefs, or felt for the intereft, or dignity of their country. A barrier was now formed, which appeared to be a lafting defence againft the intriguing fpirit of France. We forgot our loffes and fufferings in the pleafing profpect

* Mr Munroe,

that our countrymen would forever efcape her deceptive fnares. But, alas, thefe hopes have vanifhed. Subfequent events, which have lulled the fears, and impaired the energies of our countrymen, have furnifhed unhappy opportunities to the friends of France, to propagate her principles, and extend her influence, in America ; and at no period, perhaps, has their fuccefs been greater, than for the laft three or four years. What is to be the refult, cannot be forefeen.

The influence of WASHINGTON, more extenfive, perhaps, than ever one man acquired over a nation, proved, during his adminiftration, a great mean, under Providence, of fecurity againft the infiduous attempts of our enemies, and the progrefs of felf-created focieties, of the tendency of which he was aware, and gave faithful warning to his country. At a later period, the full tide of wealth, which has poured in upon almoft all clafles of citizens has operated as an antidote againft the libels of the enemies of our government. But, if thefe peculiar advantages have fcarcely preferved us from the *mortal embraces* of France; if a fteady oppofition has been made to a government whofe meafures have been uniformly fuccefsful, and murmurs, complaints and in-

surrections have marked a period, attended
with every foothing circumftance of profperity, what may we not fear from thofe
prefling difficulties which may arife, and
which, probably, will be the refult of thofe
luxurious habits we are now forming, when
the means of gratification, as they muft be,
are contracted ? What indeed can we expect
in any circumftances, fhould the fpirit of Illuminifm continue its progrefs ; fhould our renewed intercourfe with France, extend the
influence of thofe principles which have already been too fuccefsfully difleminated in
America ?

Although the obfervations in this chapter
have a political afpect, they have not been
introduced with a political defign, but in evidence of the progrefs of the genius of Illuminifm, the conftant attendant of French
influence. France is the region of Illuminifm,
and her policy and principles are dictated by its
fpirit. The leading characters in her revolution have publicly avowed the fentiments fo
induftrioufly propagated by Voltaire, and fyf-
tematically taught in the fchool of Weifhaupt.

In a difcourfe, compofed by Anacharfis
Cloots, and printed and circulated by order

of the National Convention, we find the following sentiments. " Man, when free, wants no other divinity than himself. Reason dethrones both the kings of the earth, and the *king of heaven.* No monarchy above, if we wish to preserve *our republic* below. Volumes have been written, to determine whether a republic of Atheists could exist : I maintain, that every other republic is a chimera. If you admit the existence of an heavenly sovereign, you introduce the wooden horse within your walls ; what you adore by day, will be your destruction at night."* By virtually abolishing the christian sabbath, enthroning Reason in the temples of the Deity, and by affixing to their burying-grounds the inscription, " *Death is an everlasting sleep,*" a sentiment expressive of the essence of atheism, the Convention gave the most explicit sanction to the above principles.

This is French liberty; the liberty they wish to propagate. The state of their finances required that they should be more immediate-ly active in promoting revolutions in governments, than in propagating atheism; as every revolution afforded a pretext for plunder, and for demanding contributions; but, in

* Residence in France.

the mean time, they have not been inactive in
their attempts to abolifh, what they ftyle,
" the *tyranny of heaven.*" Their Anti-Chriftian
writings, which have been rapidly circulated,
even in thefe diftant regions, and their
Propaganda, afford ample proofs of their zeal.
Girtanner, in his memoirs on the French
revolution, eftimates " the acting members of
the club of the *Propagandifts*, at fifty thoufand,
and their general fund, in 1791, at thirty
millions of livres; that they are extended
over the world; having for their object the
promotion of revolutions, and the doctrines
of atheifm. It is a maxim in their code, that
it is better to defer their attempts for fifty
years, than to fail in them through too much
precipitation."*

That the principles of infidelity have
attended the progrefs of French influence in
America, does not admit of a doubt. The
truth of this remark is evident from infpection. Who can avoid feeing, and who that
believes the importance of religion to mankind, can avoid lamenting, the alarming
revolution which has taken place here, in the
effential doctrines of natural and revealed

* Barruel's Memoirs, Vol. II. p. 245.

religion? The fentiment has not yet been openly avowed, but I have fatisfying evidence, that it has been more than once afferted, to this effect, that *we never fhould be free until the chriftian church was abolifhed.*

The two following articles of information were communicated by a gentleman of the firft refpectability in Pennfylvania, to his correfpondent in New England, who has favored me with his letter:* He writes, " On the occafion of the election of citizen M'Kean, an altar was erected on the commons, on which the ftatues of liberty and peace were placed. Large libations were poured on the altar by the priefts of liberty, who were clothed in white, with red caps, ftuck round with fprigs of laurel. After which an ox was facrificed before the altar, and its flefh divided among a thoufand citizens, while many republican toafts were drank by the company. The ox was likewife adorned with garlands, according to the Pagan ritual."

The other article is as follows: " It was lately propofed in Ricket's Circus, (at Philadelphia) to exhibit a view of *Hell*, for the di-

* The original is with the author.

version of the good company, and such exhi-
bition would have taken place, had not the
combustibles, prepared for the occasion, taken
fire too soon, and consumed the house." The
first account, the writer says, " is taken from
a democratic paper, printed at York (Penn-
sylvania) and with respect to both, he adds,
" You may rely on the accuracy of the information."

The following statement is taken from a
printed abstract of the society, for the propa-
gation of the gospel in foreign parts, for the
year, ending the 21st February, 1800, and annexed to Dr. Courtenay's anniversary sermon.

" A sect, called New Lights, but composed
of the most enthusiastic and extravagant of
the different denominations in Nova Scotia,
have lately appeared in that province, whose
political, are said to be equally dangerous with
their religious principles. It is believed that
the conductors of these people are engaged in
the general plan of a total revolution in religion and civil government ; and it is a certain
fact, that the Age of Reason, Volney on the
Ruin of Empires, and a false representation of
the French Revolution, have been secretly
handed about by professed New Lights."

CHAP. XV.

IN CONTINUATION.

IN the former chapter, fome documents were introduced to prove that the noxious weed of Illuminifm had taken root in our happy foil, and was here diffufing a poifon, more penetrating and mortal than that of the famous Bohan Upas. Let us now examine the afpect of facts, which are univerfally known to exift, and obferve their agreement with this hypothefis. If all appearances harmonize with the fentiment here advanced, and are unaccountable on every other fuppofition, this will give much additional weight to the proofs already adduced. Indeed, the evidence refulting from the exifting ftate of things, often impreffes the mind with a conviction, no lefs forcible, than the moft pofitive teftimony. This kind of evidence, however, requires an equal balance ; its due weight can never be afcertained where the unfteady hand of

T

passion holds the beam, or where prejudice
possesses the scale.

Persuaded that there are many of my fellow
citizens, who are not guided by prejudice or
partiality, I would invite them to a calm and
deliberate consideration of the following queries, founded on the state of things among us,
as they have existed, and do now exist.

1st. Whence arises the avowed attachment
of a numerous party, in this country, to
France ? Why are we constantly hearing, that
she is the only nation in whom we can repose
confidence, on whose fidelity we can rely ; the
only friend of the rights of man ? Why are all
her enormities so industriously palliated, and
her victories celebrated as the triumphs of
righteousness ?

Perhaps there has never been an instance in
the history of man, of a more sincere and dif-
interested friendship between two nations,
than that which once subsisted between America and France ; and I hope there is not now
a citizen in the United States, who would not
feel a sincere and ardent pleasure in the return
of that nation to the paths of wisdom, and
the enjoyment of the sweets of civil and re-

ligious liberty. But what muſt be in the heart
of that man, whoſe feelings accord with her
principles, and who is gratified with the ſuccefs
of her preſent meaſures ? Muſt not every
friend to ſociety, to order, and religion,
adopt, with refpect to France, the energetic
language of the Patriarch, "O my ſoul, come
not thou into their ſecret ; unto their aſſembly, mine honor, be not thou united ?"
Whence then the charm which ſo ſtrongly
binds ſuch a numerous party in this country
to France ?

Is it their malicious oppoſition * to the

* Sunday, Nov. 17, Anacharſis Cloots did homage
to the Convention, and made the following propoſal.
" It is now become an acknowledged truth, that the ad-
verſaries of religion have well deſerved of mankind. On
this account, I demand, that a ſtatue be erected to the
firſt abjuring prieſt, in the temple of reaſon." The propoſal of Cloots was referred to a committee, and adopted.

In the ſame month, on the motion of Chaumette,
which was received with applauſes, it was reſolved in the
Council of Paris,

1. That all the churches and temples of different
religions and worſhip, which are known to be in Paris, ſhall
be inſtantly ſhut.

2. That whatever troubles may enſue in Paris, in
conſequence of religious motives, the prieſts and miniſters

Chriſtian religion, burning their bibles,* obliterating the chriſtian ſabbath,† paying divine
honors to imaginary deities,‡ and counte-

of the different religions, ſhall each be particularly
reſponſible.

3. That every perſon, requiring the opening of a
church, or temple, ſhall be put under arreſt, as a ſuſpected
perſon, &c. &c."—Kett on Prophecy, London edit. 1800,
Vol. II, p. 240.

* "What," ſays an intelligent American gentleman,
in a letter to his friend in Boſton, dated at Havre, Nov. 24,
1793, "What do our good folks think of dethroning God,
burning the Bible, and ſhutting up the churches? Before
I came here, they burnt the bible in the public ſquare,
pulled down the images of Jeſus and Mary, in the
churches, and filled the niches with thoſe of *Reaſon* and
Liberty, &c. See Dr. Morſe's Thankſgiving Sermon,
1798, p. 22.

† "Oct. 25, 1793, a new calender was propoſed, and
adopted by the Convention, with a view to obliterate the
remembrance, as well as obſervance of that holy day,
which has been, from the earlieſt times, conſecrated to the
exerciſe of public devotion. Feſtivals were appointed at
ſtated periods, ſimilar to thoſe which were eſtabliſhed in
times of Idolatry, to the Virtues, to Genius, to Labor, to
Opinion, to Rewards." Kett, Vol. II. p. 236. See
alſo, Reſidence in France, p. 270, New-York edit.

‡ "The magnificent church of St. Genevieve, at Paris,
was changed, by the National Aſſembly, into a repoſitory
for the remains of their great men, or rather into a pagan
temple, and as ſuch, was aptly diſtinguiſhed by the name
of the *Pantheon.*" [N.B. *The Pantheon was a beautiful edifice*

nancing, even in their National Aſſembly, the

at Rome, anciently a temple, dedicated to all the Gods.] " To
this temple, the remains of Voltaire and of Rouſſeau were
conveyed in ſolemn and magnificent proceſſion. The
bones of Voltaire were placed upon the high altar, and
incenſe was offered. And when the infatuated multitude
bowed down before the relics of this arch enemy to Chriſt,
in ſilent adoration, a voice, a ſingle voice, was heard to
utter, in a tone of agony and indignation, theſe memorable
words ; *O God, thou wilt be revenged!* Search was immediately made for the man, who thus dared to interrupt theſe
rites, and this Abdiel was, probably, ſacrificed to the fury
of the multitude." Kett, Vol. II. p. 233.

"Previous to the tenth day, on which a celebration was
to take place, a deputy arrived, accompanied by the
female goddeſs ; that is, (if the town itſelf did not produce one for the purpoſe) a Roman dreſs, of white ſatin,
was hired from the theatre, with which ſhe was inveſted,
her head was covered with a red cap, ornamented with
oak leaves, one arm was reclined on a plough, the other
graſped a ſpear, and her feet were ſupported by a globe,
and environed by mutilated emblems of feodality.

" Thus equipped, the divinity and her appendages
were borne on the ſhoulders of Jacobins "*en bonnet rouge*,"
and eſcorted by the national guard, mayor, judges, and
all the conſtituted authorities, who, whether diverted or
indignant, were obliged to preſerve a reſpectful gravity
of exterior. When the whole cavalcade arrived at the
place appointed, the goddeſs was placed on an altar
erected for the occaſion, from whence ſhe harangued the
people, who, in return, proffered their adoration, and
ſung the *Carmagnole*, and other republican hymns of the
ſame kind. They then proceeded in the ſame order to
the principal church, in the choir of which the ſame cere-

moft impious blafphemies againft the God of
Heaven ? *

Has France recommended herfelf to our
efteem by thofe horrid murders, and fcenes
of carnage and blood, which fpared neither
the hoary head, the innocent fupplicating
female, nor the harmlefs infant, but added
wanton barbarity to her pretended acts of

mories were renewed; a prieft was procured to abjure
his faith, and avow the whole of Chriftianity an impofture:
and the feftival concluded with the burning of prayer
books, faints, confeffionals, and every thing appropriated
to the ufe of public worfhip. The greater part of the
attendants looked on in filent terror and aftonifhment;
while others, intoxicated, or probably paid to act the
fcandalous farce, danced round the flames, with an appearance of frantic and favage mirth. It is not to be
forgotten, that reprefentatives of the people, often prefided as the high priefts of thefe rites; and their official
difpatches to the Convention, in which thefe ceremonies
were minutely defcribed, were always heard with burfts
of applaufe, and fanctioned by decrees of infertion in the
Bulletin, a kind of official newfpaper, diftributed at the
expenfe of government, in large towns, and pofted up in
public places." See Refidence in France, p. 270, N.Y. ed.

* "Nov. 1793, the pupils of the new republican fchool,
of the fection des Arcis, appeared at the bar, and one of
them fet forth, that all religious worfhip had been fuppreffed in his fection, even to the very idea of religion.
He added, that *he and his fchool fellows defied God,* and
that, inftead of learning fcripture, they learned the decla-

juſtice ;* and perſecuted the miniſters of relig-

ration of rights. The preſident having expreſſed to the
deputation the ſatisfaction of the Convention, they were
admitted to the honors of the ſitting, amidſt the loudeſt
applauſe." Kett, p. 224.

* " Sept. 2, 1792. The people broke open the priſon
of the Abbaye, and commenced a maſſacre of the priſ-
oners. Many had been confined on ſlight ſuſpicions ;
many poor prieſts, on no particular accuſation, but merely
becauſe they were prieſts. The ſame horrid ſcenes were
extended to all the priſons in Paris.

Among the unhappy victims who ſuffered on this occaſion, was Madame de Lamballe, whoſe only crime was,
the friendſhip of the queen. She was ſtruck on the head
with the bludgeon of one aſſaſſin, and her head ſeparated
from her body by the ſabre of another. The body, after
a ſeries of indignities, not to be related, was trailed by
the mob through the ſtreets." Moore's Journal, Boſton
edit. Vol. I. p. 183—189.

Kett, deſcribing the ſame event, ſays, " Three ſucceſſ-
ive nights and days, ſcarcely meaſured their aſſaſſinations
of prepared victims, who had been, from motives of private hatred and revenge, impriſoned. Seven thouſand
ſix hundred and five perſons were inhumanely murdered,
and the aſſaſſins publicly demanded their wages. During
the ſhort interval between theſe bloody ſcenes, the paſſions of the populace were fired ; the relentleſs Roland
had the care of the general police ; the bloody Danton
was the miniſter of juſtice ; the inſidious Petion was
mayor of Paris, and the treacherous Manuel was procu-
rator of the common hall. Theſe magiſtrates were evidently, either the authors, or the acceſſaries, of theſe
maſſacres." Kett, Vol. II. p. 235.

ion with marks of peculiar rancor?* Or are
they pleafed with the loofe morality of
France;† where the facred obligations of the

"A fourth of thefe, our reprefentatives," fays the
author of La Conjuration, page 160, " ripped open
the wombs of the mothers ; tore out the palpitating em-
bryo, to deck the point of a pike of liberty and equality." Many inftances of the like nature might be produced, but I am not willing to torture the feelings of
the reader.

* The commiffioner Garnier wrote thus to the Convention, on the 11th of December, 1793 : " I have cauf-
ed fifty eight priefts to be drowned." The next month
he writes again, " Ninety priefts have juft been brought
to me ; I have drowned them, *which has given me great
pleafure.*" " It appears that there have been two millions
of perfons murdered in France, fince it has called itfelf a
republic ; among whom are reckoned 250,000 women,
230,000 children (befides thofe murdered in the womb)
and 24.000 chriftian priefts, many of them Proteftants."
Kett, Vol. II. p. 252.
The conflagration of 1820 towns, villages, and ham-
lets, in one portion of its own territory ; the deliberate
affaffination of women and children, by hundreds and
by thoufands ; the horrid pollution of female victims,
expiring or expired ; and the eftablifhment of a tan yard,
under the aufpices of government, for manufacturing
leather out of the fkins of the murdered citizens, are
facts, which exclufively grace the blood ftained annals of
the gallic republic, and give to the revolution a dreadful
pre-eminence in guilt." Kett, Vol. II. p. 251.

† " To keep the minds of the Parifians in the fever of
diffolute gaiety, they are at more expenfe, from the na-

marriage covenant are diffolved ;* proftitu-
tion countenanced ;† fuicide publicly applauded ;‡ where diffipation meets with no
check, and the endearing charities of life are
extinguifhed ? ‖ Do thefe perfons find the

tional treafury, for the fupport of the fixty theatres, than
all the penfions and honorary offices in Britain, three
times told, amount to. Between the 10th of Auguft,
1792, and the 1ft of January, 1794, upwards of 200
new plays were acted in the Parifian theatres. Their *im-
morality* and their barbarifm exceed all defcription."
Kett, Vol. II. p. 253.

   * " In confequence of the decree relative to marriage, it
is calculated, that, in 1793, one hundred and fifty di-
vorces took place in every month in Paris." Kett, Vol.
II. p. 253.

   † By a decree of the Convention, June 6, 1794, it is
declared, that there is nothing criminal in the promifcu-
ous commerce of the fexes." Kett, Vol. II. p. 217.

   ‡ " Beaurepaire fhot himfelf at the furrender of Verdun.
When the news reached the National Affembly, M. De-
launay propofed, that his remains fhould be brought
from St. Menehold, and interred in a French Pantheon.
This was immediately decreed, and an honorary inferip-
tion put on his tomb." Moore, Vol. I. p. 238.

   ‖ " A man, or rather a monfter, named Philippe,
came to the Jacobin club, of which he was a member ;
and, with a box in his hand, mounted the tribune. Here
he made a long fpeech on patriotifm, concluding by a
declaration, that he looked upon every one who prefer-

traits of a *great* nation in the cruel exactions
practised in Holland ; in their perfidious deal-

red the ties of blood and of nature, to patriotic duty, as
an aristocrat worthy of death ; and to convince them of
the purity and sincerity of his own principles, he opened
the box, and held up by the grey hair, the bloody and
shrivelled heads of his father and mother, which, said
the impious wretch, I have cut off becaufe they obsti-
nately persisted in not hearing mass from a constitutional
priest. The speech of this parricide received the loudest
applauses." Le Historie du Clergé François, or, History of the French Clergy, p. 328.

The following information was communicated in a
letter from a gentleman of the first respectability in Europe, to his friend in the United States, dated Sept. 1800:

" I cannot refrain from mentioning another particular. A Count Soden, proprietor of lands on the borders
of the Black Forest, has several small Iron Works on his
estates, which occasioned him to be continually riding
from place to place during the stay of Jourdan's army,
in that country, in 1796. He published, at Nuremburg,
an account of his own observations. He had many
transactions with the different detachments who ravaged
that country, so that he was perfectly acquainted with
the state and conduct of that army. He says, that to
keep the army always in good humor, there was a fund
for a theatre, and concerts of music, and balls, at every
head-quarters, and that a liberal allowance was granted
to the officers who took with them their wives and mif-
treffes. Each had as many bed fellows as he could support by his plunder. The ladies, of course, were the
patroneffes of every gaiety and elegance. But lying in,
and particularly, nursing, was altogether incompatible

ing with the Swifs ; or the deteftable arts by
which Geneva was fubjugated to her will ?
Has fhe recommended herfelf to Americans
by her determination to plunder us of our
property ?* By her meditated attack on the
fouthern ftates,† or by thofe unprovoked dep-

with this plan of the National Councils. The only remedy for this, which occurred to their wifdom, was *(her-*
refco referens !) to *drown the new born infants,*——to
DROWN THEM ! ! ! This was actually done under military
efcort. A ferjeant and party of foldiers accompanied
the murderers, and protected them from the peafants.
Count Soden did not fee any of thefe facrifices with his
own eyes, but he faw two of the innocent victims, and
he heard feveral of thefe accounts in a way that he could
not doubt of their truth. In particular, he faw a clergyman, at a village about 12 Englifh miles from Nuremburg, who being alfo a magiftrate, attempted to hinder
the perpetration of the horrid deed. The foldiers threw
him into the river, and fired fome fhots at him and at
thofe who faved him. He was fo fortunate as to fave
the little innocent, and took it to his houfe and provided
a nurfe for it. The mother went away next day, with the
reft of the party, but ftaid feven weeks at a little town
five miles off, and in all that time, never once fent
to inquire whether this iffue of her own blood was dead
or alive. All this is publifhed by Count Soden, and his
name affixed as a voucher for the truth of it. I defy the
annals of human debafement to match this."

* See Barlow's Letter, March 1, 1798.

† Harper's Addrefs of March 2, 1799.

redations on our commerce, condemned by a
moſt reſpectable member of their legiſlature,
as equally inconſiſtent with good faith, and
found policy ?*

Not admitting the above as the foundation
of their attachment to France, her partiſans
will probably rather recur to their uſual plea,
which, however deſtitute of ſubſtance, has a
more reputable aſpect, viz. gratitude, yes
gratitude, never to be cancelled, for her afforded protection.   It is no ſmall trial of patience to be compelled to anſwer pleas, which
have no foundation in reaſon, nor even in the
mind of the perſon who makes them ; and
which are brought forward merely to conceal
leſs honorable ſentiments.   It is very eaſy to
anſwer in the preſent caſe, that if gratitude
is ſtill due for aſſiſtance, for which the ſtipu-
lated price has been paid in full, and which was
afforded, as every one muſt be ſenſible, and as
the National Aſſembly have acknowledged, not
from a regard to the intereſts of republican-
iſm, but from oppoſition to England, this
gratitude is due to the ancient, and not to
the preſent government of France ; and ought
to lead us to deplore the fate of an unhappy
king, and not to attach us to thoſe who, with

* Paſtoret's motion in the Council of 500, 1797.

circumstances of needless and unfeeling cruelty, have deprived him of his crown and life.*

Or will they justify their partiality for France by the plea, that it is a *sister republic*; the land of liberty? It is styled, indeed, a republic, but in reality, a more despotic government does not exist in Europe. From the beginning of the revolution the people have been the dupes of successive factious leaders, who have misled one part by false representations, and drove the other by terror into a compliance with their ambitious views. But now, their government is in theory, as well as practice, despotic. However favorable to the natural rights of men, we may believe the several constitutions successively adopted in the years 1791, 1793, and 1795, to have been, the present leaves the people but a very faint semblance of representation or legislative power.

U

* Among many instances in confirmation of this fact, it is sufficient to observe, "that the head of the princess Lamballe was hoisted on a pike, and carried before the temple where the royal family were imprisoned, and they were called to the window to see it. A fainting fit, from hearing of the event, fortunately saved the queen from the heart-rending sight." See Moore's and Clery's Journals.

Are we not then warranted in presuming, that, among the more enlightened citizens, at least, the real grounds of attachment to France, are different from the ostensible ones?

2d. To what other cause, than the one here suggested, can we ascribe that opposition to all the leading measures of the late administration, which has been uniformly maintained by those identical persons, who have manifested such a strange predilection for French politics? The notoriety of this opposition, renders it unnecessary to adduce any proofs of its existence. That our rulers have committed errors, is presumable. They were human beings, and had to explore a new, and untried path, amidst innumerable difficulties, without the useful aid of precedent and experience. But were those errors such as afforded any just pretext for the perpetual clamors, the factions, cabals, and insurrections, with which they have been opposed, and impeded? Whatever may have been their errors, the result of their measures has been the establishment of peace with the nations of Europe; peace with the Indians upon the principles of humanity, and with prospects of permanency; the preservation of our neutrality against artful and violent attempts to involve us in European con-

tentions ; the confolidation of our feeble
union, and the reftoration of that vigor and
energy which were almoft exhaufted. Our
deranged finances have been reduced to a regular fyftem, and a revenue raifed, which,
though fcarcely perceived in its operation, has
been adequate to the fupport of government,
has anfwered many extraordinary demands,
and effected a confiderable reduction of the
public debt. To the fame judicious fyftem,
are we indebted for the exiftence of a *Navy*,
which has enabled us to repel many wanton
encroachments on our neutral rights, and
been the principal means of our prefent com-
mercial profperity. Favorable arrangements
were alfo made for the recovery of our property from the hands of fpoilers ; and that this
provifion has not been more complete has
probably been owing to the belief which the
French government entertained of their influence in the United States. With great juft-
nefs, Prefident JEFFERSON announced, in his
inaugural fpeech, that our government, at
the clofe of our late adminiftration, was " in
the full tide of *fuccefsful* experiment."

I fhall not attempt a further juftification
of thofe meafures which have been fo feverely
cenfured. All who have witneffed the difficul-

ties from which we have been extricated; and
the prosperity which has resulted to all classes
of citizens, from the measures which have
been adopted and pursued, in the two late
administrations, and yet remain unsatisfied,
as to their wisdom, I can have no hope of
convincing by any arguments I can use. It
ought, however, to be remarked, that these
measures were adopted by WASHINGTON and
ADAMS, and warmly recommended by them,
as indispensible to the peace and prosperity of
the United States, and the perpetuity of their
union and independence. We may probably
soon be called to witness the effects of a departure from their salutary system.

To what cause then are we to attribute the
opposition which has been made to such men,
and such measures; men, who have given the
most unequivocal proofs of a wise, patriotic,
and faithful adherence to the principles of rational liberty, and the interests of America,
through scenes which try men's principles;
measures, which have procured to this country, respectability abroad, and prosperity and
strength at home? The nature and systematic
operations of this opposition appear perfectly
unaccountable and mysterious, unless we recur
to some *secret* influence. This influence, mov-

ing many hidden springs, produces thofe uni-
form effects which are vifible in all parts of
our country. And this conclufion forces itfelf
upon our minds when we recollect, that the
clafs of men who raife this outcry, and who
are fo extremely jealous of any encroachments
on the privileges of mankind, are the very
perfons who juftify all the extravagant and
tyrannical proceedings of the French government ; not excepting that arbitrary act of the
directory, in 1797, which drove into banifhment, without the form of a trial, fome of the
beft of her legiflators, and the moft worthy of
her citizens.

3d. Whence is it, that this jealous concern
for the liberties of America, this nice fenfe of
the rights of man, (to which is afcribed the
oppofition to government) originated in the
fouthern States, is ftill moft prevalent there,
and is thence communicated to the eaftern
States ? I certainly have no difpofition to foment a fpirit of divifion, nor would I fuggeft
an idea detracting from the refpect due to
many fouthern gentlemen, whofe fortunes
have been devoted to the purfuits, not of
pleafure, but of the liberal arts, and who have
become bleffings and ornaments to their country ; but, as an oppofition in principles is

known to exist, it becomes necessary, in order
to acquire just notions of liberty, that the
origin and tendency of these principles should
be freely discussed. Some observations on the
subject are evidently of importance in the
present inquiry. I must, therefore, take the
liberty of asking, if the principles, which have
attached many of the citizens of the United
States to France, and rendered them opposed
to the leading measures adopted by Washington and Adams, flow from an enlightened
spirit of freedom, whence is it, that these sentiments are found, originally, and principally,
in the southern part of the Union ?

Are the habits and manners of the people
there, more congenial to the spirit of genuine
republicanism ? or are the citizens generally
better informed ? Do they acquire this patriotic spirit in their elective assemblies, where,
we have been informed, by one of their own
legislators, that bludgeons are substituted for
proxies, and the arguments of the citizens
acquire weight in proportion to their bodily
strength and activity ? In drawing the portrait of a true republican, would you represent
him with one hand contending for the rights
of man, and with the other holding a scourge
over his trembling slaves ?

It has been fuppofed of the firft importance in republican governments, that the lower claffes of the people be well informed ; that youth be taught to fubject their paffions to the dictates of reafon and duty, and be early trained to habits of virtue, induftry, and economy. But if, as has been reprefented, New England be the " *La Vendee* of America," and its inhabitants ariftocrats, until they are politically regenerated by the fouthern ftates, the above principles of education muft be renounced as erroneous, and the race ground, and the gaming table, acknowledged the beft fchool for the education of republicans.

Here new paradoxes occur, and paradoxes they remain till we recollect, that Illuminifm firft dawned upon the fouthern ftates ; that they formed the principal refort for European emigrants, and there only, we difcover the lodges which derive their origin from the *Grand Orient*, at Paris. Have we, then, no grounds to conclude that thefe outrageous pretenders to liberty, who " difpife government, and are not afraid to fpeak evil of dignities," are the genuine offspring of that fect, which we have feen alike oppofed to the reftraints of religion, and the laws of fociety ?

Why do we hear, from the fame quarter, the clergy of New England reprefented, not only as ufelefs, but a public nuifance.* I fhall not undertake the defence of this order of men, nor attempt a refutation of the various, and very indefinite charges brought againft them. The people of New England are acquainted with their clergy, and can judge for themfelves, whether or not they are juftly cenfured. One charge, however, as it is more frequently alledged, and refpects their fecret intentions, and therefore not fo eafily refuted, demands more particular attention. The charge to which I refer, is, in fubftance, this, that they are unfriendly to the political interefts of their country, and the principles of the American revolution. Is this a fact? If it be proved, I prefume it muft be by the fame kind of logic, by which thofe who bring the charge, attempt to prove that WASHINGTON was blind to the interefts of his country ; ADAMS, a monarchift ; and the citizens of New England, ariftocrats. But let us attend to facts.

* In proof of the fact here intimated, I beg leave to refer the reader to thofe newfpapers in which Wafhington's fyftem of politics is condemned, and the meafures of France advocated in the grofs.

It is a matter of public notoriety, that at the time of the American revolution, no clafs of men were more united, or more active in their efforts to promote that caufe. Their public performances afford, alfo, abundant proofs of their warm attachment to the French revolution, until it became evident that the caufe in which France had embarked, was the caufe of licentioufnefs, oppreffion, and atheifm. Have then thefe men in a body relinquifhed that fyftem of political faith, which, at that period, they fo fervently embraced? To what probable caufe, can fuch a general revolution of fentiment be attributed?

Their accufers will not probably afcribe it to their ignorance, for they likewife accufe them of meddling too much with politics; it is therefore prefumable that they have, at leaft, acquired political information.

Will it be faid that the profpects of ambition have led them aftray? This would be a very uncharitable fuppofition indeed; for although they are *men of like paffions* with others, they are not, in all cafes, expofed to *like* temptations. Excluded, by their profeffion, from pofts of worldly honor and profit, they are merely fpectators of the contentions of ambition. Unless they are influenced by a patriotic concern for their countrymen, they have no connection with government, other than to secure for themselves the blessings of freedom, and to transmit the precious inheritance to their posterity. In haste to deprive them of public confidence, their accusers have industriously, and indiscriminately applied to the clergy here, the charges brought against the order in Europe. But what similarity in situation is there between the cardinals, bishops, and lords spiritual, of the European hierarchies, and an American clergyman, who, by the scantiness of his support is compelled to the most rigid economy, and often to labor with his own hands, to obtain a decent support for his dependants ; and instead of the prospect of preferment, must consider himself fortunate if he be not dispossessed of his office, and subjected to the inconveniences of a removal ?

Their poverty, indeed, exposes them to temptations, in point of property, should such temptations present ; but it is fortunate, with respect to this charge, that the public measures to which they have conscientiously given their support, have been unfavorable to their private interests. The duties of imposts and excife, which are taken from the confumer, and the eftablifhment of banks, which has operated greatly to `advance the price of every article of life, have reduced their means of fubfiftence. This has been fo obvious, that their parifhioners, in general, have felt themfelves bound in juftice to increafe the nominal fum, to preferve the original value of their ftipends. The clergy, alone, are excluded a fhare in the increafing wealth of their country ; and were they governed by felfifh motives, merely, would be the firft to oppofe, rather than the firft to defend the adminiftration.

But it has alfo been fuggefted, that, in efpoufing this caufe, they have meanly courted the favor of the majority. For an anfwer to this charge, facts declare the truth ; for it is a known fact, that many of the clergy have nobly maintained their fentiments, and warned their hearers of their danger, at the hazard of their difpleafure, and of offending particular gentlemen of influence. The author in particular, pleafes himfelf, that he, at leaft, fhall efcape the charge of a time-ferver, as he is weekly notified, through the medium of the Worcefter Gazette, by one high in office, that the caufe he here advocates, is faft finking into contempt; and that he already foreſees the " downfall of Federal Clergymen."

The above obſervations are not ſo much deſigned to vindicate the clerical order, as to develope the real deſigns of their calumniators. Theſe accuſations appear as groundleſs as the attachment of their authors to French politics. It is to be preſumed that they are not the real cauſes of the preſent oppoſition to the clergy of New England. No; their attachment to order, the reſiſtance they make to the progreſs of philoſophiſm, their exertions in defence of Chriſtianity, and their attempts to impreſs its important, but unwelcome truths, on mankind, conſtitute their real crime, in the judgment of their accuſers. Political opinions prove a convenient cover for ſchemes not yet ripe for execution. Were the enemies of religion among us to come forward unmaſked, and avow their real deſigns, it would be demonſtrative proof that they had apoſtatized from the principles of their maſter; but the diſciples of Voltaire and Weiſhaupt are true to their favorite maxims, " to bind men with *inviſible* bands. To ſtrike, but hide the hand."

We accordingly find thoſe who are endeavoring to deprive the clergy of all public confidence, abounding in what D'Alembert calls "*bows to religion.*" Religion is carefully fpoken of with high refpect, in thofe publications which denounce the body of the clergy as hoftile to the interefts of their country. "They muft be gained or ruined," the reader will recollect, is a prime maxim of the order ; but finding that the clergy of New England will not be induced to betray their religion and country, and confign themfelves and their pofterity to infamy and wretchednefs, they are unceafingly reprefented, as attempting to fubvert thofe eftablifhments to which they have invariably given their fupport, and to annex to their office the honors and emoluments which are peculiar to the corrupt religious eftablifhments in Europe.

That friends to order and religion, by a feries of mifreprefentations, are led to give their fupport to fyftems, which, if free from deception, they would detect, is not to be doubted ; but the man who approves the principles on which the French revolution has been conducted, and is pleafed with that liberty and independence, which have received the fanction of the National Affembly, cannot but wifh for the abolition of the Chriftian faith, and whatever gives it fupport.

W

The reader will remark, that the fame
evidence which proves that Illuminifm, or
French influence, (for one involves the other)
has exifted in America, proves that it now
exifts among us. The fimilarity of the effect,
indicates the famenefs of the caufe. In 1794,
we find Fauchet fketching the grievances
which excited the weftern infurrection. In
1797, appeared the focieties of United Irifhmen. In the fame year, the American Envoys
were affured, " That it was in vain for them
to think of uniting their countrymen againft
France, by expofing the unreafonablenefs of
their demands. You ought to know," they
are told, " that the *diplomatic skill* of France,
and the *means she possesses in your country*, are
fufficient to enable her, with *the French party
in America*, to throw the blame which will
attend the rupture of the negociations, on the
federalifts ; and you may affure yourfelves
this will be done."*

At the fame period, Mr. Pinckney was told
by another French negociator, " we know we
have a very confiderable party in America,
who are ftrongly in our interefts."† Has this

* Difpatches from American Envoys, publifhed by the
Secretary of State, No. 2.

† Ibid. Exhibit A. No. 4.

" French party in America," this " very confiderable party," on which the Directory
placed fo much dependance in 1797, became
entirely extinct ? Have they been in no
degree active, fince that period, to excite
jealoufies, foment divifions, alienate the citizens from their beft friends, to diffeminate
the principles of infidel philofophy, and overturn the ancient happy eftablifhments of our
country ?

If, in their attempts to deprive us of our
religion, they have not obtained an equally
decided victory, zeal has not been wanting,
nor has their fuccefs been inconfiderable. The
principal bulwarks are yet fafe. Our bibles are
not configned to the flames ; nor our places
of worfhip devoted to idolatry, and pagan
rites. The Chriftian fabbath, although treated
with practical contempt by fome who ought
to give it their firm and decided fupport, is
not yet abolifhed by law. But many of the
outworks are in the power of the enemy, and
they are daily making regular and alarming
approaches.

It is not my intention, by the foregoing obfervations, to implicate all thofe who err in
their political opinions, as engaged in the con-

spiracy against Christianity, and social order.
This is far from being the case ; yet I have no
doubt that many persons, who are sincere
friends to religion, their country, and mankind, are led, by a series of misreprefentations,
to give their support to systems, which, if seen
in their true nature and tendency, would excite their abhorrence. It is, indeed, astonish-
ing that good characters, real friends to Chriftianity, should be so easily filled with suspicion
and jealoufy towards men of established character, for piety, talents, and patriotism, and
drawn in to aid the enemies of their religion,
and their country ; and this too, by persons,
whose moral and religious characters they cannot
but hold in abhorrence ; but Weishaupt himfelf wondered at the success of his own policy,
and in his confidential epistles, often exclaims,
" What cannot men be made to believe."

Perfuaded that many are unwarily led to
advocate a caufe which militates against the
beft interests of their country, these historical
sketches, and articles of evidence, have been
collected for their benefit ; and with the fame
friendly defign their calm and unprejudiced
attention is requested to the contents of the
following

ADDRESS.

Friends, and Fellow Citizens,

I am very fenfible that the difcerning eye will
difcover many defects in the foregoing ftatement, but they are errors of the head, not of
the heart. There is not a circumftance inten-
tionally mifreprefented, nor a fentiment expreffed, which is not the refult of conviction.
I am aware that fome from policy, and others
from fentiment, will be difpofed to treat thefe
apprehenfions as chimerical; but to me they
are real. In my view, alarming dangers
hang over my country, and even now the
lurking foe is preparing an explofion, which,
unlefs prevented, will level her rifing glories
with the duft. Poffeffing thefe fentiments,
neither duty nor patriotifm would fuffer me
to decline a fervice, however ungrateful,
which afforded fome profpect of aiding a caufe
to which I feel myfelf connected by the ftrongeft ties of affection. Your country, is my
country; here I have a family, dear to me,
and friends, whofe fortune, with my own, is
connected with that of America. Can I then
fee her dangers, and be filent?

W 2

Warmly has my heart entered into the pleasing prospects which have dawned upon the land of my nativity, nor will I yet despair of her salvation, confiding in that helping hand, which has been her guide in darkness, and her shield in danger. Numerous and powerful still are her friends, could they be roused to exertion ; and exertion there must be, or our ruin is inevitable. If propitious heaven has decreed salvation for our country, means will be found to dispel the facinating charm which is now drawing her into the ravenous jaws of her devourer. She will be enabled to distinguish *real* from *pretended* friends. While we are supine and indolent, resting in the goodness of our cause, and fondly hearkening to those who cry peace and safety, the enemies of our peace, of our independence, of our religion, are alert and restless. It is painful and alarming to hear worthy citizens applauding themselves for the sagacious discovery, that the commotions of the day are merely agitations excited by contending candidates ; that we are all aiming, in different ways, at the same object; " that we are all federalists, all republicans." These sentiments, industriously propagated by those who wish to lull us into security, unfortunately accord with that love of ease, so unhappily prevalent in our most important concerns.

Under a like paralytic ſtupor, the effect of French intrigue, and modern illumination, the Helvetic republic fell a prey to her treacherous invaders. " The inhabitants ſeemed fearful of being rouſed from their indifference, and were offended at predictions meant to put them on their guard. Woe to him who diſturbed the general quiet by peeviſh reaſoning on the future, and on the danger of connections in which they were ſinking deeper and deeper ! The majority of the Swiſs were like thoſe patients who are angry with the phyſician for deſcribing their diſorder to them."* " We come among you as friends. We are your brothers. Do not be afraid of any ill treatment. Property and perſons ſhall be protected, as much as the enemies of liberty ſhall be made to ſuffer."† This was the language of Mengaud, commiſſioner of the Executive Directory, in his proclamation, prefaced with "Peace and ſafety to all his friends." The too credulous Swiſs greedily drank the luſcious poiſon ; they believed that the Direc-

* Mallet Du Pan's Deſtruction of the Helvetic Republic, Boſton edit. 1799. p. 108. A book that ought now to be read by every American.

† Ibid. p. 256.

tory were, what they pretended to be, friends
to freedom, and the rights of man. They
even banished their faithful monitor, when he
endeavored to awaken them to a sense of their
danger. But " *imprisonments, insults, rapes, requi-
sitions,* and *rapine* of all kinds, signalized the
arrival of these strangers, whom *Mengaud* had
but just announced to their victims *as brothers
and friends.*"*

Confide not, my countrymen, in an imaginary power to resist the subtle invaders, when
once they have bound your hands with invisible bands. Your enemies themselves have
forewarned you, " that an army of *principles*
will prevail, where an army of *soldiers* cannot."†
When they have sufficiently corrupted your
morals, philosophized your religion, overturned
your ancient establishments, and disseminated
their disorganizing principles among you, then
will they rise upon their prey, and add America
to the list of " *fleeced*" republics.

Mallet Du Pan, describing the situation of
Switzerland, previous to the late revolution

* Mallet Du Pan's Destruction of Helvetic Republic,
P. 147.

† Thomas Paine.

there, obferves, "There was no State in Europe fo fecure from the contagion of French
principles ; every thing was an antidote to
this peftilence : The flow and phlegmatic
character of the inhabitants, their rooted and
powerful habits, the experience of a government adapted to their difpofitions ; and, in
fine, the foundnefs of their judgments, which
guarded them againft the feductions of the
pen, and of the tongue." If fuch examples
will not teach, nor fuch warnings alarm us, our
ruin is not far diftant.

It is a falfe and dangerous fentiment that
" monàrchies alone have caufe to dread the
revolutionizing fpirit of the times ;" for it is
obvious that republics are the theatres on
which political mountebanks moft fuccefsfully
exhibit their diforganizing feats. Where, as
in fuch governments, popular elections are frequent, and the poifon which infects a diftant
member, is inftantly conveyed to the vitals.
When an individual is gained, a lodgement is
made in the government, of which that individual forms a part, either in perfon, or by his
agent ; and his influence is inftantaneoufly
felt. In monarchical governments it is very
different. The difeafe, which there pervades
the external parts, but very remotely affects

the vital, active powers of government. How
feeble the impression which France was able
to make upon England, compared with the
shock which the republics of Europe received
from her revolutionary agents? The combination of *United Irishmen*, and similar societies in
England and Scotland, produced no visible al-
teration in the British government; but had it
been similar to the American, a complete
revolution must have been the consequence.

The same cause which renders republics
more accessible to these evils, proportionably
prevents their suppression; for those dangerous persons form directly or indirectly, that
very power on which society depends to expel
the foe; and hence, the government, in
this respect, is reduced to a nullity. Nor is a
large number of conspirators necessary to
raise obstructions and impede the government; for in every society these persons find
many natural allies, ever ready to join their
forces. Such are disappointed candidates,
who are commonly willing rather to impede
and perplex, than to assist their more successful
competitors; such are those, and they are not
a small party, who, from a natural jealousy of
their rulers, are prepared to credit every
unfavorable intimation concerning them,

however improbable or abfurd. Such, in fine, are thofe felfifh beings, whom no confiderations of public good will induce to act with any vigor : Thefe, if they do not appear in direct oppofition to government, are fo many clogs and impediments to its vigilance and activity. Thefe plain obfervations are introduced to awaken you, my countrymen, to that virtuous watchfulnefs and firmnefs, neceffary to preferve a free government, and to put you upon your guard againft the diforganizing arts of thofe, who, under whatever pretext, are endeavoring to overturn the fyftems and eftablifhments which experience has taught you are ufeful.

Do you afk, what is to be done ? As uncommon abilities and penetration are lefs ufeful in a fearch after happinefs, than upright intentions and an honeft heart, I fhall attempt an anfwer to the fuggefted inquiry. The ingredients of mental and focial happinefs, like the neceffaries of life, confift in fimples, and are eafily obtained. When the theorizing geniufes of the day have invented a better medium of refpiration than the vital air, or a bodily aliment preferable to that which nature provides, then will they merit a hearing, while they promife us a *Utopia* in the regions of infidelity, and quiet repofe on the billows of a revolution. But if you wifh for that kind of order and quietnefs, for which our favored land has been diftinguifh-ed, the following directions point out a plain and fafe path.

1. Attend to the education of your children, and let it be your principal care to imprefs their minds with religious and moral truth. Much has been faid, and much more might be pertinently faid, upon the import-ance of education. The youthful mind is a field prepared for the reception of precious feed; but if neglected, will foon be overfpread with every poifonous growth. I am con-vinced that faithful endeavors to inftil the principles of virtue and religion into the minds of youth, is attended with a much greater probability of fuccefs than is ufually imagined. It is undeniable, that early im-preffions, which have appeared to be entirely erafed by the influence of ftrong paffions and peculiar temptations, have furvived the fhock, and produced the happieft effects. Even where this is not attained, early habits of regularity, decency, and induftry, are not of fmall importance in fociety, nor are they eafily loft. The impreffions made by fuch an educa-

tion have evidently had a great effect in preventing the influence of the diforganizing principles of the day, in the New England ftates.

A religious education was formerly repro- bated by infidels, under the pretence that it gave a bias to the mind before the judgment was matured ; but they themfelves have removed this objection ; they are not afhamed to make it a maxim in their code, to feize the young, untutored mind, and infufe into the unfufpecting heart the poifon of atheifm. Learn from your enemies the importance of early impreffions, and while they are attempt- ing to diffeminate the feeds of infidelity, let it be your watchful care to introduce the vigorous plants of piety and virtue. Furnifh their minds with ufeful knowledge ; teach them the true dignity of man ; read to them the leffons of experience, habituate them to felf government, the regulation of their paffions, and a ready fubmiffion to needful reftraints. Attend to their books, and exclude the numerous publications which are either fecretly, or avowedly, defigned to propagate the immoral and irreligious fpirit of the times ; or, if this is not practicable, let them not be without the antidote furnifhed in

x

many late able replies to the pleas of infidelity. We deny our profession as Christians, if it is not our first concern, in the education of our children, to impress their minds with the fear of God; to establish them in the principles of natural and revealed religion, and the evidences of the Christian faith.

The task of forming the youthful mind, at all times one of the most important duties in society, acquires, in present circumstances, an increased demand on our attention. Religion, society, parental affection, unite in the demand. It would be happy, if present dangers should prove the means of awakening the attention of the Christian world, to a subject so deplorably neglected.

It is fervently to be hoped, in particular, that our Colleges, and other literary institutions, will be preserved from contamination. These are principal objects in the view of the modern enemies of mankind. In observing the weaknesses of human nature, they have discovered, that a youth of genius, thirsting for literary fame, whose education was unfinished, and his judgment immatured, was precisely in a situation to be impressed with the fascinating charms of Illuminism, and prepared to exchange his underſtanding and confcience, for the flattering title of a philofo-pher. Much depends, at this day, upon the gaurdians of our public feminaries, and much we expect from their fidelity and zeal, in preferving theſe public fountains from im-purities.

2. Support thoſe inſtitutions of your an-ceſtors, which you have feen crowned with peace, glory, and happinefs. When will mankind receive the inſtruction fo forcibly impreſſed by univerfal hiftory, by daily obfer-vation, and the word of God, that " *Righteouf-nefs alonee xalteth a nation?*" That rank atheifm is deſtructive to fociety, receives a ready aſſent from thoſe who appear infenfible of what is equally true, that a departure from the habits and principles of ſtrict virtue and religion, is an approximation to atheifm, and a departure from the only folid foundation of focial order and peace. They forget that it is religion, not in theory, but in practice, which conſti-tutes the happinefs of an individual, and of a nation.

Men who derive their importance from fhowy accomplifhments, and the gewgaws of life, look with contempt upon the fimple man-

ners of our venerable ancefters ; but whatever
advancements we have made in ufeful difcoveries and the elegant arts of life, juftice
requires that we afcribe to their virtues our
moft precious bleffings. In a ftrict attention
to family government, in early habits of induftry, in a fincerity, fimplicity and temperance of manners, and in the civil, literary,
and religious eftablifhments of our country,
they laid the foundations of what remians of
glory and ftrength in the American edifice.
We do not afcribe to them perfection. Human
nature will be attended with the characteriftics
of weaknefs. In them, a zeal for the truth
degenerated into a degree of intolerance ; but
have not we rufhed with violence into the
oppofite and more dangerous extreme ? The
narrow path of virtue is ftretched to an
almoft unbounded width ; and in thefe days
of catholicifm, the idea that infidelity dif-
qualifies for public offices, or even for future
happinefs, is condemned as a fpecies of bigotry.
It is eafy to perceive that fuch a relaxation of
moral and religious principles is, in its effects,
a near approach to atheifm. The checks
neceffary to reftrain the ftrong corruptions of
the heart are taken away, and thefe corruptions, as they gain ftrength, gradually undermine, and, in their progrefs, will demolifh the
ftrongeft bulwarks of fociety.

When an individual loofes his habits of induftry, acquires a relifh for expenfive living, and feeks in fcenes of diffipation that fatisfaction which he no longer finds in the fober pleafures of life, we forefee his ruin, and withdraw our confidence ; and can a fociety compofed of fuch individuals, be long profperous and happy ? No ; the ruin is more inevitable in the latter cafe, than in the former ; for a profligate individual may be controled, perhaps reformed, by his fober neighbors, but when vicious manners become prevalent in fociety, a current is opened which defies all reftraint, and carries along with it, many who nobly attempt to refift its impulfe.

I am painfully confcious that the puritanic fimplicity of our anceftors, will rather excite a fneer of contempt, than a defire of imitation in this felf-important age. Enjoying the full tide of profperity, moderation, temperance, and the reftraints of religion, are unwelcome themes : But this, my countrymen, is the alternative eftablifhed in the high unalterable decrees of Heaven, if we participate the *vices* which have wrought the ruin of other nations, we muft alfo partake of *their plagues !*

It will doubtleſs be underſtood that theſe
obſervations are not deſigned to recommend
any particular uncouthneſs of manners, which
the cuſtoms of the age, or their peculiar circumſtances produced. The value of a gem is
not diminiſhed by a poliſhed ſurface. What
principally demands our attention and imitation in our worthy progenitors is, their love
of religion, and their ſtrict practical regard to
its duties, producing undiſguiſed ſincerity,
and genuine patriotiſm. Religion gave direction, vigor, and activity to all their meaſures. Religion firſt generated, and that alone
can preſerve, the glory of America.

Guard this treaſure with peculiar care.
Here let it be remembered, the efforts of your
enemies are ſecretly, but powerfully directed;
and never will they feel their victory complete until, as they themſelves expreſs their
hope, " *Chriſtianity is thrown into the back
ground.*" To this object they are equally
prompted by their enmity to the holy nature
of this religion, and by a deſire to extend
their influence over the mind; for they cannot be inſenſible, that while virtue exiſts in
the world, their ſyſtem muſt meet oppoſition.

But what are the conſiderations by which
theſe men would induce us to renounce a

religion, of the authenticity and benign influence of which, we have such convincing
proofs ? Modern infidels appear to have
placed their principal dependance on the articles, *priestcraft* and *prejudice*.

Under the *first*, they paint, in glowing
colors, the pride, ambition, and oppreffions
of the papal hierarchy, and of the higher orders in other religious eftablifhments. That
the emoluments, injudicioufly annexed to the
clerical office in many parts of Europe,
fhould induce men, deititute of religion, to
affume the facerdotal character, is perfectly
agreeable to the known principles of human
nature ; and that fuch men, when in office,
fhould difregard their folemn engagements,
is very probable ; but the conclufion thefe
modern reafoners deduce from thefe premifes,
viz. That the Chriftian religion is a fyftem
of prieftcraft, is not fo clear. If, by afcribing
religion to priefcraft they mean, that thefe
wicked priefts invented the religion taught in
the gofpel, the abfurdity of the idea, muft be
apparent to every perfon acquainted with its
holy, humble doctrines. It could not be *craft*,
but the higheft degree of ftupidity, in fuch
men to invent a religion, which, in the
ftrongeft terms, condemns their ambition, and
holds them up to mankind as impoftors.

If they mean, that the miſconduct of ſome of its miniſters and profeſſors proves that Chriſtianity is a fable, the inference is equally erroneous ; for is it evident, that if revelation be true, hypocriſy would have had no exiſtence, or that ambitious men would not make religion a ſtepping ſtone to preferment ? Yet until it ſhall be proved that wicked men would not thus pervert a true religion, this perverſion of Chriſtianity, is no argument againſt its divinity. Is gold leſs valuable becauſe it has been counterfeited ; or, becauſe *Thomas Paine* pretends to reaſon, is reaſon a uſeleſs faculty ? If your bibles countenance hypocriſy, pride, and oppreſſion, they are unworthy your regard ; but while they inculcate nothing but what is virtuous and praiſe worthy, bind them to your hearts, faithfully follow the directions they give, and they will lead you to ſafety and happineſs.

Another inſtance of modern ſophiſtry is, to reſolve religion into prejudice, and conſtantly uſe theſe terms as ſynonymous. This is a moſt popular ſtroke. It is infallible with men of weak minds, who would be thought *philoſophers*. The very ſound of vulgar prejudices frightens them out of that pittance of judgment which was theirs by original inheritance.

But is this a fact, that mankind are biaffed in favor of doctrines which ftand oppofed to all the ftrong, leading paffions of the heart? Univerfal obfervation teaches, that we are apt to be prepoffeffed in favor of what we wifh to be true ; but the modern doctrine of prejudices, contradicts this obfervation : it reprefents mankind as unaccountably difpofed to believe, in oppofition to the dictates of reafon, and the impulfe of inclination.

That Voltaire, after writing forty volumes againft Chriftianity, and fpending feventy years in attempting to " *crufh the wretch,*" fhould be tormented by prejudices in favor of religion, may appear credible to thofe who " believe in all unbelief ;" but in this, and many fimilar inftances, every unbiaffed mind will fee a fuperior power impreffing the foul with an irrefiftible confcioufnefs of Almighty juftice.

Not the arguments in fupport of Chriftianity, but thofe of an oppofite nature owe their influence to the power of prejudice. Thefe deceivers are not unmindful of the oppofition of the heart to the reftraints of religion. On this principle, corruption of morals becomes an important part of their fyftem. They ftudioufly endeavor to inflame the paffions of

men, that the obligations of duty may become more irksome ; and that the cause they
wish to support, may find a more powerful
advocate in the heart.   Infidelity owes its
strength, not to argument, but to feeling.
An hundredth part of the evidence which
has been produced in support of the truth of
Christianity, would determine every person's
judgment, in all cases, where the inclinations
had no influence.

My countrymen, suffer not the arts of sophistry, or your own passions, to rob you of that
benign religion which was so dear to your
ancestors, which supported them under their
trials, rendered their names precious to posterity, and originated establishments so happy
in their effects.

3. Consider the importance of having your
public offices filled with men of virtue and
religion.   This is indeed included in the example of your ancestors ; for they had the
wisdom to discern, that none but those who
were friends to religion, were friends to
society ; but the present alarming inattention
to this subject, recommends it to more particular notice.

Are magiftrates the minifters of God, and the reprefentatives of the Supreme Ruler ? Thus *Chriftians* are taught to confider them. When, therefore, a nation, nominally Chriftian, elect to thefe offices, men avowedly, or practically oppofed to the Chriftian religion, is it not a public affront to the righteous Ruler of the univerfe ? However cafuifts may determine this queftion, the afpect, which the election of fuch men has upon the intereft of fociety, is in every refpect highly unfavorable. A perfon of this defcription, may faithfully ferve his country, or he may betray, or he may enflave it ; what courfe he will take, depends merely on circumftances. A regard to reputation, and what is called principles of honor, which might have an influence in fmaller concerns, ceafe to operate when the high objects of ambition are prefented to the mind. When a man of ambition comes within the reach of fupreme power, its attraction overcomes the influence of thofe weaker motives which, for a time, held him within the fphere of duty. In thefe circumftances men of principle only, fuch as was the Jewifh Moses, and the American Washington, and Adams, will remain in their proper orbit, fuperior to all attraction, but that of their country's good.

To pretend that a man diſtitute of the principles of religion, will be as likely to be faithful to the intereſts of his conſtituents, as one of an oppoſite character, is to deny that religion tends to the good of ſociety. But have the oaths of office, a belief of the being and perfections of God, and of a future ſtate of rewards and puniſhments, no influence to excite men to fidelity ? We know they are nothing to him who believes, " *that death is an everlaſting ſleep,*" but they cannot fail to operate on every mind which is not paſt feeling.

It is futile to attempt to juſtify an inatten-tion to the characters of thoſe we elect to office, by pretending, that to ſerve the pur-poſes of ambition, men may aſſume a char-acter which does not belong to them. It is not eaſy for thoſe who are objects of public notice, to conceal, for a long period, their ruling paſſion ; and were ſuitable caution uſed, it is not probable that a deception would fre-quently take place. In any event, this cannot juſtify inattention to the ſubject. Shall we, with our eyes open, truſt our deareſt intereſts with a knave, becauſe it is poſſible we may be deceived in the man we believe to be honeſt ? Our utmoſt care to preſerve our dwellings may prove ineffectual, but shall we therefore put fire to them ?

When due care is taken to elect men of good principles to public offices, even if the electors are deceived in the man of their choice, the object is not wholly lost. The character of the Supreme Ruler is duly respected ; the public suffrage is on the side of virtue, and virtuous men are countenanced ; wickedness suffers a public frown, and the person elected, perceiving that he owed his advancement to a virtuous character, will be more careful to support such a character ; and temptations to neglect, or betray his trust, will have less effect upon him ; but when irfidelity is no bar to promotion, or when virtue and religion are considered as of no importance in a public character, these reftraints are removed, and every temptation operates with full force.

When men, deftitute of the principles of religion, are raifed to important public offices, the effect muft be extremely pernicious, as it refpects the interefts of religion in fociety. You are not now to learn what influence examples, and efpecially the examples of the great, have on the general ftate of manners

Y

and society. The temper of such men will influence their manners. However they may adopt some of the forms of piety, from a regard to appearances, their immoral and Anti-Christian feelings, will give a complexion to their whole deportment.

I do not hesitate to say, that the man, with whom these considerations have no weight, is a stranger to the nature, excellence, and importance of Christianity, and has the heart of an infidel. You will not, my countrymen, unless you are fatally blinded to your own interests, suffer the glare of abilities, or the impulse of a party spirit, to allure you to commit the interests of your country to men, who are enemies to those principles which form the pillars of society.

Our inattention to the choice of public officers is highly criminal. Many entirely neglect the right of suffrage, while others bring forward the name which chance, or some one more designing than themselves, presents to them. What should we say of a ruler who should make choice of his principal officers in the same careless and capricious manner? Neither an individual, nor a multitude, ought to have the disposal of the affairs of a nation, who is not more attentive to its interests,

Greater electioneering zeal is not, indeed, neceffary than appears in fome parts of our country ; but it is fervently to be wifhed, that this zeal were lefs under the impulfe of party fpirit, and that calm, difpaffionate citizens would make it a more ferious object to difcover, and introduce into public offices, characters, whofe election might promife profperity to their country.

4th. Beware of men, who feek to rob you of your liberties and religion, by flattering your paffions, and by a pretended concern for your interefts. This is not a new mode of deception, but, in common with other modes, has undergone a modern refinement. Marat, the greateft incendiary in France, Dr. Moore obferves, " addreffed the mob in the ftyle of a lover to his miftrefs ; and the motto of a Journal, which he publifhed, was " *Ut redeat miferis, abeat fortuna fuperbis,*" that is, " *Take the money from the rich, that it may be reftored to the poor.*"

As a guard againft the influence of ambitious, popular men, the Athenians provided the fentence of oftracifm. Each citizen was required to write on a bone the name of the perfon, in his eftimation, the moft popular ;

and he whose name was found on the greatest
number of bones, was banished from the
Commonwealth, under the idea, that he had
acquired an influence dangerous to the republic. However absurd in itself, and cruel in
its operation, this practice was, it discovered
a due sense of the danger arising, in a free
government, from the ascendency ambitious
men may acquire, by flattering the populace,
and gaining the direction of their passions.
While there are corrupt, ambitious men, this
kind of influence will exist, and will be principally found in those governments where its
operation is most pernicious. Not, however,
in ostracism, but in virtuous habits, and a
watchful attention to the interests of the public, shall we find our safety from the arts of
those insidious foes.

To confound the reputation which is the
result of faithful services, and approved merit,
with the popularity of an impostor, is as injurious to the public, as to individuals. The
former is as beneficial, as the latter is destructive. A small degree of discernment, duly
exercised, is generally sufficient to detect the
insincerity of those who flatter but to destroy.
If I may be indulged a quotation so unfashion-
able, I would say, that St. Paul has accurately

described thefe deceivers ; " They *zealoufly* affect you," fays he, " but not *well* ; yea, they
would exclude you, that ye might *affect them.*"

The man who lives only for himfelf, while
he pretends a deep concern for the interefts of
fociety ; the fomenter of factions ; the feeker
of offices; the corrupter of morals ; the avowed enemy of Chriftianity ; the man who endeavors to irritate your mind, by reprefenting
neceffary public expenfes, as an act of opprefi-
fion, and thofe reftraints which the order of
fociety requires, as tyrannical ; in fine, he who
addreffes your paffions, rather than your under-
ftandings, fuch men bear the genuine characteriftics of impoftors ; and are either the deluded
agents of a party, or have themfelves defigns
which they wifh to conceal, while they pro-
claim themfelves the advocates of the rights
of man.

5th. Attend to the fources from which you
derive your political information. The diforganizers of Europe were not unmindful of
the advantage to be derived to their caufe from
having public preffes, and periodical publications, under their direction. There, however,
a degree of caution was neceffary, and an ap-
prehenfion of confequences gave a check to

the licentiousness of the press ; but in the United States, this medium of imposition is, in a great measure, unembarrassed ; and demands very serious attention. Excepting the salutary restraints imposed by the *Sedition Bill*, those who were disposed to foment divisions, excite jealousies, and disunite the people from their government, have had an opportunity of incessantly attacking the minds of the citizens with the grossest misrepresentations.

Evils of great magnitude have already originated from this source of mischief. Objects have been presented to the public, under every possible circumstance of distortion, and suspicions excited which were entirely groundless. It is an outrage upon common sense to pretend, that there has been any adequate cause for the clamors and opposition which have embarrassed the measures of the late administration. Could the citizens of the United States have an impartial view of their proceedings, it is to be presumed, that ninety-nine hundredths of the virtuous, enlightened part of the community, would cordially approve of what, by the influence of misrepresentation, many are now led to reprobate.

An effectual remedy for the abufes of the prefs has not yet been difcovered, and perhaps, in a free government, no other remedy can be confiftently reforted to, than the virtue and good fenfe of the citizens; and this, we have reafon to fear, will be but feeble indeed. The prefent ftate of the public mind is evidently calculated to increafe, rather than diminifh, the evil.

If, my countrymen, you will calmly and difpaffionately inquire after truth, means of information are not wanting. If you give no encouragement to the numerous productions of the day, which are plainly dictated by a defire, not to inform your judgments, but to inflame your paffions, they will ceafe; but while your minds are open to fcurrility, calumnies, and falfehoods, they will abound. A fpirit of party has given currency to many publications, from different quarters, which ought never to have feen the light. Truth is more injured than affifted, by an alliance with paffion. Important truths are not, indeed, to be fuppreffed, becaufe they may irritate the enemies of truth; but groundlefs afperfions, and needlefs provocations, fhould meet your pointed difapprobation, if the falvation of your country is dearer than the fupport of a party.

It is not the defign of thefe obfervations to diffuade you from an attention to public affairs. Your country needs, and has a right to demand, your vigorous efforts. It adds an additional fhade to the darknefs of the prefent day, that, where the ftimulus of party fpirit does not operate, there is fuch a degree of torpor and inattention to a fubject in which the happinefs of millions is involved. A neglect of public intereft muft be viewed as criminal in any ftate of fociety, but more efpecially where the people claim to be the fources of honor and authority. But let your exertions be given to your *country*, not to a *party*; and being convinced that religion, morals, order, and a government of laws, are the pillars of your national profperity and peace, let thefe have your firm and vigorous fupport.

6th. Renounce the Anti-Chriftian and irrational practice of " fpeaking evil of dignities." " Thou fhalt not fpeak evil of the ruler of thy people," is one of thofe divine precepts which commends itfelf to every man's confcience by its evident propriety, and demands our attention as of prime importance to the order of fociety. It is an evil to which free governments are peculiarly expofed; and a ftrong propenfity in human nature to this evil, has given an advantage to the diforganizers of the prefent day, which they have not neglected.

The impracticability of fupporting the authority of the laws, and the energy of government, when the executors of thofe laws, and the officers of that government, are objects of conftant fcurrility and abufe, muft be obvious to every perfon of the leaft reflection. The experience we have had of this fpirit among ourfelves, is furely fufficient to fatisfy us of its pernicious tendency ; and under a change of adminiftration, it is painful to fee many indulging the fame fpirit, which they have fo juftly reprobated in others. In the perfon, conftitutionally invefted with authority, we are to contemplate, not the *individual* whofe election we once oppofed, however reafonable and well founded that oppofition may have been, but the *magiftrate*, in fupporting whom, on conftitutional ground, we fupport the government of which he is the head.

Even when the public good requires, as doubtlefs it may require, that the character and conduct of public officers fhould be expofed, a folemn decency, and not a bitter and

licentious spirit, still less a spirit of falsehood,
ought to mark the transaction. Nor will the
censurable parts of their conduct justify our
withholding aid, countenance, and support in
the due execution of their office.

7th. Seriously reflect upon the nature and
tendency of secret societies. Weishaupt himself proposes the question, " Have you any
idea of the power of secret societies ?" It is
obvious, at first view, that they are not
friendly to that harmony and cordial union
which are so desirable in every society.
Should some of the children in a family form
themselves into a secret club, exclude their
brethren from their private meetings and confidence, and be often whispering their secrets;
it is easy to foresee that an undue partiality
among the confederated brethren, and jealousy, distrust, and alienation of affection on
the other part, would be the natural consequences. The effects will be similar, and
equally certain, though they may be less vis-
sible, in larger societies. From the notorious
tendency of such combinations, many weighty
and interesting objections were made to the
establishment of the order of the *Cincinnati*; but
the development of the mysteries of Illuminism, has given an additional weight to these

arguments, and placed, in a glaring light, the dangerous tendency of exclusive confederacies.

I am not insensible that these remarks criminate, in a degree, the order of Masonry. The respect I feel for many gentlemen of this order, a . . . my acquaintance, who I doubt not, ... society with pure intentions, and . . . . this contamination ; and my . . . . corruptness of the New England b . . . . have made it, to me, an ungrateful . . . . . . to relate the dark defigns to which this order, after fo long preferving its luftre, has been fubjected. I can affure them that views, to which every private confideration muft yield, have been my fole inducement to undertake this duty. This, in the minds of thofe of the order whofe approbation is moft to be valued, I doubt not will appear a fufficient apology. To thefe candid Mafons I hefitate not to fay, that to me, a fufpenfion at leaft, of mafonic operations, appears to be a meafure, which the fafety of fociety, in its prefent ftate, recommends ; and it is difficult to conceive how any perfon, who admits the truth of the foregoing ftatements, can diffent from this idea. It is the fentiment of many refpectable Mafons ; and feveral lodges in Germany have actually

clofed their proceedings, on this principle. It
is with pleafure I tranfcribe an extract from
a mafonic oration on fuch an occafion, hoping, that the example and the fentiments,
will have their due influence.

"Brethren and Companions, give free vent
to your forrow ; the days of innocent equality are gone by. However holy our, myfteries
may have been, the lodges are now profaned
and fullied. Brethren, and companions, let
your tears flow ; attired in your mourning
robes attend, and let us feal up the gates of
our temples, for the profane have found means
of penetrating into them. They have converted them into retreats for their impiety,
into dens of confpirators. Within the facred
walls they have planned their horrid deeds,
and the ruin of nations. Let us weep over
our *legions* which they have feduced. Lodges
that *may ferve* as hiding places for thefe confpirators muft remain forever fhut, both to us
and every good citizen."*

He who thus facrifices his amufements and
pleafures to the interefts of fociety, acquires a
dignity beyond what the higheft honors of
Mafonry can confer.

* Barruel's Memoirs, Vol. IV. p. 63.

8th. Cheerfully submit to the reftraints which the rules of religion and the good order of fociety require. There are principles in the human heart which unwillingly endure control, and on thefe principles the diforganizers of the day place their chief dependence. They artfully endeavor to inflame the paffions, to awaken a defire of forbidden objects and gratification, and then exhibit the reftraints of religion and government, as tyrannically oppofing enjoyment.

This is the true import of *liberty and equality*, as the words are ufed by modern impoftors. The abufe to which thefe terms are liable is obvious; for, when once unlawful paffions are excited, it becomes an eafy tafk to perfuade men that whatever checks thofe inclinations, is an abridgment of their natural liberty; and when, in this way, a popular torrent is formed, in vain religion, order, juftice, or humanity oppofe their reftraints. *Liberty* is a vague term, nor do thefe men wifh to define it; they wifh to have men feel that they are injured by whatever oppofes their inclinations, and when they have inftilled into them this fentiment of fedition, it is eafy to render men hoftile to all the reftraints which religion and focial order impofe. This is the liberty which

z

Illuminism has actively propagated. Modern
philosophers have discovered, that the laws of
modesty impose an unjust restraint on the
freedom of the fair sex; that the subjection
which children are required to yield to their
parents, is an unreasonable usurpation; and
the law which obliges married people to live
together, after their affections for each other
are alienated, is tyrannical.

But you, my countrymen, do not wish for
this kind of liberty. The glory of your constitution is, that it preserves the citizens in
the free enjoyment of their natural rights,
under the protection of equal laws and impartial justice. You wish to have your lives,
property, and privileges, both civil and
religious, preserved to you: Guard then those
of your neighbors; for know, that the moment the enclosures which protect their rights
are broken down, yours are no longer secure.
Whatever weakens the force of moral and
religious obligations; whatever lessens the
restraints, already sufficiently weak, which the
laws impose on the unruly passions of men,
proportionably exposes the lives, liberties, and
property of the quiet part of the community
to the depredations of the lawless.

One of the moft furprifing effects attending
the diforganizing principles of the day, is,
that men of property fhould be induced to
give fupport to a fyftem which deftroys the
barriers by which property is protected. That
fome few, who wifh to acquire influence, and
mount into places of honor and truft, fhould
adopt thefe violent means to " burft open the
doors" leading to the emoluments of office, is
not, indeed, ftrange; but the quiet, unambitious
citizen, whofe utmoft wifh is to preferve the
fruit of his labor and exertion, muft be completely duped not to perceive, that he expofes
to the greateft hazard what he is principally
defirous to preferve. Pleafed with the idea of
faving a few fhillings, neceffary for the defence of his property, he expofes the whole.

In the fame abfurd manner do *they* reafon,
who conceive that the perfection of liberty
confifts in unbounded indulgence. Extremes
are faid to meet and produce fimilar effects.
This maxim applies to the prefent cafe. When
people grow weary of fubjecting their paffions
to neceffary reftraints, a ftate of diforder and
faction enfues. Some popular leader, improv-
ing his afcendency over the divided, diftract-
ed multitude, erects a defpotifm ; and, flattering their paffions, he at length eftablifhes his
authority on a furer bafis.

Read this truth in the history of ancient Greece and Rome. See it verified in modern France. Advancing, in their own opinion, to the very pinnacle of liberty and equality, we see them suddenly reduced to a state of complete vassalage. The discerning part of the nation were not deceived, but weary of a liberty which left no security to their lives or property, they acquiesced in the usurpation of the Chief Consul : This is the natural and unavoidable consequence of licentious indulgences. Hearken not then, my countrymen, to those, who endeavor to render you dissatisfied with the restraints of religion, or the expenses necessary for the maintenance of useful institutions, and the support of good government.

TO THE CLERGY.

AS this subject is particularly interesting to the AMERICAN CLERGY, I beg leave to present it to them in a point of view, in which it appears to me of peculiar importance.

Fathers and Brethren,

WHILE I see with pleasure your exertions in opposition to prevailing infidelity, permit me to direct your attention to a temptation, by which, as we learn from the preceding historical sketches, the German divines were ensnared, viz. that of attempting to reconcile infidels to the gospel, by reducing it to their taste ; either by explaining away, or keeping out of sight, its offensive peculiarities. From the foregoing recital it appears, that the second branch of Illuminism, the German Union, was grafted on a mutilated system of Christianity.

In the history of the Christian church, we are often reminded of the injuries Christianity has received from the attempts of its advocates to render the gospel palatable to its

Z 2

oppofers. Upon this principle, firft the Oriental,
then the Platonic, afterwards the Ariftotelian,
fyftems of philofophy became, in different
ages, the ftandards for explaining the facred
writings ; and the doctrines of Infinite Wifdom have been diftorted into a compliance
with thofe fyftems of human weaknefs and
folly. Hence, alfo, arofe the fcheme of an
hidden meaning, and myftical interpretation,
fo zealoufly adopted by Origen and others.

This doubtlefs has been fometimes done with
a friendly defign, but the confequences have
always been unhappy ; and unhappy they ever
muft be. Befides the impiety of the attempt,
it is very obvious, that it is merely the corruptions, in thefe mutilated fyftems, with which
infidels harmonize. Their hearts are no
more reconciled to the *Gofpel* than before ; all
the advantage refulting to Chriftianity confifts
in the external aid they afford the caufe ; and
this is incomparably overbalanced by the in-
jury done to the purity of its doctrines. Nor
is even this aid now to be expected ; for modern infidels, renouncing their former pretended refpect for natural religion, have taken
their proper ground, which is abfolute atheifm.

" Thus did not Paul." While fully fenfible that the gofpel he preached was. " a

stumbling block to the Jew, and foolishnefs to the Greek," he complimented neither the one nor the other, either by adopting their fentiments, or relinquishing his own ; but with a refolution worthy the great defender of Chriftianity, determined, in face of this oppofition, to affert the doctrine of a crucified Saviour ; nay, as if forefeeing the indirect meafures which fome would take to recommend Chriftianity, he pronounces " him accurfed who fhould preach another gofpel," adding, that by *another gofpel*, he meant the gofpel of Chrift perverted, or corrupted.

In this he conformed to the will of his Divine Mafter, who ftated unalterably the terms of admiffion into his kingdom, declaring with the greateft folemnity, that unlefs they received the kingdom of God (the fcheme of doctrines he taught) with the meeknefs, and teachablenefs of little children, they fhould in no wife enter therein. It will not be pretended that he was unmindful of the oppofition of the human heart to the doctrines he taught, but under a full view of that oppofition, he demanded for them a ready reception, and the unequivocal fubmiffion of mankind. The triumph of the gofpel is effected not by relinquifhing its demands, in compliance with the corruptions and caprices of mankind, but by ſubduing the pride, enmity, and oppoſition of the heart, and " bringing into captivity every thought to the obedience of Chriſt."

I have thus, my countrymen, expreſſed my ſentiments with the freedom which is *yet* one of the happy privileges of our country ; and with the faithfulneſs which becomes one who ſees his fellow men expoſed to iminent dangers, I have never covered a paragraph, on any of the ſubjects here brought into view, by an anonymous publication. By this obſervation I mean not to criminate, in the leaſt degree, thoſe gentlemen, who, in this way have enlightened and inſtructed the public ; but it is moſt agreeable to my feelings, eſpecially in preſent circumſtances, to make myſelf reſponſible to the public, for my opinions on theſe ſubjects.*

* Had the proper names of the authors been affixed to all the publications of the day, it is to be preſumed that the clergy would be found chargeable with a ſmall proportion of thoſe which have been ſo liberally palmed upon them without the leaſt evidence, and plainly with a deſign to injure their characters.

Confidering the fpirit of the times, a meaning and defign will doubtlefs be attributed to
the writer which never entered his mind.
With refpect to himfelf, this is a circumftance
of trifling confequence ; as it refpects the fuccefs of his labors, he is defirous to remove
every obftacle ; and would therefore obferve,
that nothing has been introduced into this
work but what, it was conceived, would ferve
to give weight to the directions fuggefted in
this addrefs. In your attention to thefe fentiments confifts your ftrength. Your enemies
muft draw you from this ground before they
can prevail. BELIEVE IN THE LORD YOUR
GOD, SO SHALL YOU BE ESTABLISHED ; BE-
LIEVE HIS PROPHETS, SO SHALL YE PROSPER.*

* 2 Chronicles, xx. 20.

CONCLUSION.

PAINFUL has it been to me, and no lefs
fo, I prefume, to the reader, to traverfe thefe
regions of moral death, and to contemplate
the direful effects produced by torrents of corruption, flowing from the fulnefs of the human heart. Gladly would I relieve his mind,
and my own, with brighter profpects and
more cheerful fcenes ; and fuch prefent themfelves to him who meekly receives the inftructions of his Maker, and furveys futurity
with an eye of faith. By this light we difcover, that the plan of Providence, however
complicated its operations, is but one ; having for its benevolent object, the production
of order out of confufion, of good from evil.
Under the government of Infinite Wifdom
and love, this confoling truth is exemplified
in numberlefs inftances, from the plant, which
owes its vigor to putrefaction, to the increafing purification the good man derives from
conflicts and fufferings ; and from thence to
the crofs of a Saviour which gave life to the
world. If we admit this prime truth, we
need not a fpirit of prophecy to forefee, that

thefe efforts of infidelity will prepare the way for, and haften its deftruction : That the convulfions excited by thefe diforganizers will (but not in the way which they predict, nor according to their intentions) purify its conftitution, and introduce an healthier ftate into fociety : That all the attempts which have been made to deftroy the foundations of moral obligation, and the evidences of Chriftianity, will eventually eftablifh the one, and confirm the other.

Is it afked when this happy era will com- mence ? Not perhaps in this theorizing gen- eration ; not while men's heads are filled with the idea of erecting a peaceful, happy repub- lic upon the bafis of atheifm. But the time will come, when wifdom will refume her feat, and man will fubmit to be taught by experi- ence, and by his Maker. Then will his ear be opened to the leffons of wifdom, to the demonftrations of truth, which the hiftory of the prefent period affords.

Would it be extravagant to affert, that the collected hiftory of all ages and nations, facred hiftory excepted, does not furnifh fo much important and ufeful inftruction, as will probably be derived from the events which

have come into view within the last sixty
years? In the period referred to, we have
been presented with what may be considered,
as a course of experimental lectures on religion, morals, and the interests of society; in
which many important principles and truths
have received a clear illustration, and been
demonstrated to the senses.

In many excellent treatises has Christianity
been defended, and the tendency of infidelity,
in its influence on the mind, and on society,
held up to the public; but as abstract reason-
ings make but a faint impression on the great
body of mankind, infidels have confidently
denied the charges brought against them,
and the justness of the conclusions drawn
from their sentiments. Infidels have formed
the minority in every society; they were
therefore naturally led to plead for *toleration.*
Their principles were under a continual check,
and a regard to reputation and personal safety,
induced a compliance with the customs and
manners of the age. In proof of the importance of religion to a civil community, the
advocates of Christianity appealed to the state
of society in heathen nations; but this did
not amount to a fair experiment; for the
heathens were not infidels. The scattered rays

of revelation, collected by their philofophers, produced fomething like a fyftem of religion, which, however inadequate to the principal purpofes of religion, had a happy effect on fociety and morals.

Infidelity never before appeared in her proper character. Infidels, formerly, fpake much of virtue and religion, applauded the morality of the gofpel, and affected to admire many of its doctrines. Lord Herbert calls "the Chriftian, the beft religion." Lord Bolingbroke reprefents " Chriftianity as a moft amiable and ufeful inftitution, and that its natural tendency is to promote the peace and happinefs of mankind." It was plead by the advocates of Chriftianity, that whoever had any real love to moral beauty could not but embrace the gofpel; but deifts denied the truth of this affertion, and to fupport their argument, were perpetually proclaiming the beauty of virtue and natural religion. But now it appears that all this was a mere fineffe, adapted to conceal the fatal tendency of their opinions. Infidelity, confiding in her ftrength, and the increafing number of her advocates, has now laid afide her mafk, and we have feen her in France, fierce, cruel, unjuft, oppreffive, abandoned and profligate, as fhe is; rejecting thofe

A a

moral precepts fhe once profeffed to admire, proudly affuming entire independence, and ranking the fovereign of heaven with the tyrants ofthe earth.

We have grounds to expect, that the genuine tendency, both of infidelity and Chriftianity, as they refpect fociety, will be fully and undeniably demonftrated. It is undoubtedly a part of the fcheme of Providence, to lay open the human heart, and to prove important truths by convincing experiments. Were mankind duly impreffed with that view of the tendency of infidelity, which late events have exhibited, it would afford a rational hope that its reign would foon ceafe; but while fo many remain unconvinced, there is reafon to fear its more deplorable prevalence, before the dawning of that happy day, when Chriftianity, infufing its benign influence into every heart, fhall produce permanent peace, and the precious fruits of univerfal love.

F I N I S.